D0206344

Queen for a Day

Pitt Poetry Series

Ed Ochester, Editor

Denise Duhamel

Queen for a Day

Selected and New Poems

University of Pittsburgh Press

HOUSTON PUBLIC LIBRARY

R01212 48294

Published by the University of Pittsburgh Press, Pittsburgh, Pa. 15261

Copyright © 2001, Denise Duhamel

All rights reserved

Manufactured in the United States of America

Printed on acid-free paper

10 9 8 7 6 5 4 3 2 1

ISBN 0-8229-5762-0

The publication of this book is supported by a grant from
the Pennsylvania Council on the Arts.

for Nick

Contents

New Poems

Smile! (1993)

Mr. Donut

They tumble from closing bars into here.
Uninspired men nicknamed for their hair:
Whitie, Red; the bald one, Flesh.

What a way to save to go to Europe.
But that's what I'm doing,
the donut waitress taking advantage
of drunks. I look through
the fatty blurred window,
remind them often of my aspirations,
drum on the countertop: I am not like them.

Red's got a novelty passport
and motions me over. He thinks
his finger's alluring as Cape Cod,
the farthest I bet he's ever gone.
"Guess where I've been?"
he slurs and has me open the blue book.
A rubber jack-in-the-box penis pops out.

I think of adding sugar to the diabetics' coffee
when they laugh, describing their naked wives.
Twenty-four hours, any day, they know here they can.
There's not even a lock on the Mr. Donut door,
so when there's a fight on the corner, Flesh tells me
to call the police from the phone in back:
"If the bikers see you finking, they'll get your ass."

From behind the muffin case, the motorcycle clash
looks like a home movie: skipping loops, a volume lapse
as bikes are kicked over, heads smashed.
The blood puddles slowly, graying.
Connie strolls in, her lipstick all crazy:
the fight's over her. She wants a light.
I know she'll stain the rim of her cup.
But they all leave big bills under the saucers,
and I get to read the few
quiet hours before dawn.

Sometimes the First Boys Don't Count

Walking home through the woods from the movie at the plaza
that I didn't remember minutes after it ended,
an action adventure that I didn't want to see, but said yes to
just in case you held my hand, and you did.
Walking home by the shortcut, the path
the developers made because they'd be building houses soon,
we had nothing to say. It was our first date
and you stopped to kiss me, the cold of the mud
wetting my feet. Your tongue, like an animal's,
rough and eager, through the chain link of a zoo's fence.
I didn't know you, but you put your hands up my shirt
like it was nothing to either of us.
You cupped each of my breasts as though holding me back,
or measuring me for something, then kept walking,
not taking my hand anymore. Even at fifteen,
I knew you were the type that after the first kindnesses,
the honeymoon was over. Your face in the night
was even flatter, less pronounced than it was in the light.
I knew, before this, that I didn't love you or even want
to talk to you the next day in school.
I told my girlfriends that you weren't very smart. You took shop
and fixed cars with your dad, not even the intricacies
under the hood, just body work. And when I went to that garage
in your backyard because we were going to another movie
and your mother said I should get you
so we wouldn't be late, I saw calendar pages curling under a picture
of a topless woman in short-shorts. She was holding a wrench
to her lips. Your dad looked at me the same way you did,
but that was how I wanted to be looked at then—that was how
I thought it should be. You washed the grease from your hands,
wiped your brow with your forearm and were ready. A few dates later
I held your penis as though it were a science experiment
and put it in my mouth when you asked. A kind of aspic squirted out.
I swallowed like a brave girl, taking her medicine.

Bulimia

A kiss has nothing to do with sex,
she thinks. Not really. That engulfing, that trying to take
all of another in for nourishment, to become one with her, to become
part of her cells. The way she must have had everything she wanted
in the womb, without asking. Without words,
kisses have barely the slurp-sound of a man entering a woman
or sliding back out—neither movement with even the warning of a bark.
The Greek word "boulimia," ox hunger.
Petting, those kisses are called, or sometimes necking.
She read this advice in a sex manual once: "Take the man's penis,
slowly at first, like you are licking melting ice cream
from the rim of a cone." But the gagging, the choke—
a hot gulp of tea, a small chicken bone, a wad of gum grown too big.
That wasn't mentioned. It's about what happens in her mouth
past her teeth, where there is no more control, like a waterfall—
or it being too late when the whole wedding cake is gone:

she orders one from a different bakery this time, so no one
will remember her past visits and catch on. She's eating
slowly at first, tonguing icing from the plastic groom's feet, the hem
of the bride's gown, and those toothpick points that kept them
rooted in pastry. She cuts the top tier into squares,
reception-like. (The thrill she knew of a wedding this past June,
stealing the white dessert into her purse, sucking
the sugary blue gel from a napkin one piece was wrapped in.
She was swallowing paper on her lone car ride home,
through a red light, on her way to another nap
from which she hoped a prince's kiss would wake her.)

The second tier in her hands, by fistfuls, desperate
as the Third World child she saw on TV last week, taking in gruel.
Her head, light like her stomach, is pumped up with air.
She can't stop. She puckers up to the sticky crumbs under her nails.
Then there are the engraved Valentine candies:
CRAZY, DREAM GIRL, ACT NOW, YOU'RE HOT. She rips open the bag,
devouring as many messages as she can at once.
They all taste like chalk. She rocks back and forth.
She has to loosen the string on her sweatpants, part of her trousseau.

The bag of candy is emptied. The paper doily
under the cake's third layer, smooth as a vacuumed ice-skating rink.
What has she done? In the bathroom, like what happened

to the mistakenly flushed-away bracelet, a gift
from her first boyfriend—the gold clasp unhooking
as she wiped herself, then, moments too late, noticing
her naked wrist under the running water of the restroom
sink's faucet . . . She's learned it's best to wait ten minutes
to make herself throw up. Digestion begins at this point,
but the food hasn't gotten very far. As ingenious as the first
few times she would consciously masturbate, making note of where
her fingers felt best, she devises a way to vomit
that only hurts for a second.

She takes off her sweatshirt and drapes it over a towel rack.
Then she pokes a Q-tip on her soft palate. Keeping in mind
the diagram in her voice class, the cross section
of the mouth showing each part's different function,
the palate—hidden and secret as a clitoris.
The teacher's mentioning of its vulnerability, split-second
and nonchalant like a doctor and his tongue depressor.
It's a fast prayer—she kneels in front of the toilet.
Her back jerks and arches the way it might
if she were moving her body to meet a man's during intercourse.
She wipes what has sprayed back to her chest,
her throat as raw as a rape that's happened to someone else.
She cleans the seat of the bowl with a rag, and cleans
her teeth with a second toothbrush she keeps for this purpose.
Her sweatshirt back on, she goes to the kitchen
to crush the cake box into a plastic garbage bag.
And leaves to dispose of it, not in the trash can downstairs,
but in a dumpster way on the other side of town.

Reminded of My Biological Clock—
While Looking at Georgia O'Keeffe's *Pelvis One*

(*Pelvis with Blue,* 1944)

I see so many things, a primitive ring,
a nest with a fallen-out bottom,
a white rubber band snapped into blue.
But mostly it's real memory
and the doctor holding up my X-ray
to the screen of light, a mini drive-in.
The bone was mine—big, oblong
and intact, even though my skin was purple,
my muscles sore. I'd fallen
off of Matthew's ten speed.
There were whispers that my hymen was probably gone,
first broken by the crossbar
that separates a boy's bike from a girl's,
rather than by Matthew himself. And now the X-rays
were showing my ready pelvis, an empty hammock,
just waiting for a sticky fetus sucking its thumb.
"It's beautiful," the doctor said
admiring my illuminated centerfold skeleton
before he turned to me, the real—and therefore
less interesting—thing. He smiled:
"You have the perfect hipbones, miss,
for carrying babies." To my mother he said,
"If everything else inside her is OK, someday
she'll be in labor for no more than an hour."
I was thirteen and I wanted no baby,
only a boyfriend, only some petting.
I wasn't even sure how I felt
about tongues. My favorite game was
swimming deep underwater, kicking through
a tent of spread legs, scissoring my thighs
in short quick ups and downs so I wouldn't lose
by booting someone in the crotch.
"But I don't want a baby," I might have said aloud.
My bone was a whorl in an X-ray-gray storm.
My disembodied pelvis, like a melted Hula Hoop.

"The women in our family are all Fertile Myrtles,"
my mother explained later. "When I got
pregnant with you, I think I was just
looking at your father," she said as emphatically
as if she were telling me the truth. So I found out how to get
a diaphragm and pills and foams and condoms and used them
all at once, memorizing the percentages
of their individual effectiveness: 80, 82, 89.5.
"I'm pregnant, I just know it,"
I would panic every month.
Exasperated, my first real boyfriend would remind me,
"Impossible. We didn't even have intercourse last month.
Remember? You were too nervous." In the meantime,
my girlfriends, one by one, skipped their periods.
There were trips for abortions or quick marriages.
One young mother left high school
to become a cashier at the Stop & Shop.
While she was still nursing, she leaked milk
through her shirt and smock, leaving
something like a perspiration spot
every time a baby cried in her line.
This wasn't for me, though I felt guilty,
my pelvis being the right shape and all.
My mother watched her talk shows, sometimes
on the topic of childless women, and muttered,
"How can those career ladies be so selfish?
If they don't have babies now,
they'll grow old and die alone."
Sometimes in my dreams I'm back on Matthew's bike,
not falling this time, but riding off
into the orange-cowboy sunset. Other times,
though, a crown of thorns sprouts in my belly—
my nightmare grows dark.
It is always daylight around Georgia's *Pelvises*.
The sky is the blue that the child she might have had
might have seen when he was first born.
Sometimes I dream bluebirds land on my hipbone

as though I were a round limb
on a desert tree. I feed them anything
they desire. Then the mother birds
feed their youngsters, and I tell them
they can stay as long as they like.

From Lorca's Deli, New York City

The cashier who usually winks at me was watching the hanging TV over my shoulder—*Kojak* or something like that. And a cat sat on the counter. A little boy was asking for cigarettes for his mother when I heard a gunshot, a little loud, I thought, for a TV. Then no, it can't be. On Avenue B the first bullet missed, but as I turned to the window the second one got him and a man went soaring and flopped onto the sidewalk as though it were his bed and he'd had a long day. The little boy was looking, too, out through the door where his head only reached *Pull* spelled backwards. He started screaming when the cashier said, "Hey, I know that guy," and I had to stop the little boy from running out to the street where a mob was forming. The assailant ran and took a right onto the block where I live, and others began running, too.

It was only five in the afternoon—a mother would send a boy to the store. We heard more distant shooting, then the squealing ambulance, cop cars in the rain. The police moved a little tired, a little afraid. One came into the deli asking, *What did he look like?* Hispanic, male, jean coat. I ventured 5'8", but added that I'm really a bad judge of height. The cashier said nothing about this guy looking familiar and the little boy just wanted to go home. The policeman said, "Little man, why don't you give us a few minutes to find the bad guy before you come on outside." So I bought this boy a 25-cent bag of yellow buttered popcorn, lifted him up onto the counter where he sat and stroked the cat. We both watched through the glass, and he said it was OK now, that it was kind of like watching TV.

What Happened This Week

(May 1, 1992)

Billy didn't come to school Tuesday,
the day his essay was due.
Instead the police showed up—
a Dragnet team—asking if anyone
had seen him since Friday.
The class huddled at the implications
of the words: missing person.
Billy, eighteen, too old for milk cartons,
but just ripe for the morgue
and a numbered tag around his bare toe.
Just ripe for a knife, a bullet,
a bat. He was gentle, small enough to be raped
then stored in a car trunk
if there was time, or left on a subway platform
with his empty wallet by his head.
When I called his mother the next day
the phone didn't ring a full ring before she picked it up.
Not having slept, she couldn't remember her address
when I said Billy's English class
wanted to send her a card.
She said Billy was the first of his family
to go to college. I told her he wrote
beautiful essays, then I said, "I mean, he *writes*
beautiful essays," trying to keep him alive
by using present tense. When he showed up
to class on Thursday, we all thought we were seeing
his ghost. Blue bruises tinted his black forehead,
like a halo collapsing inward.
He said he'd been arrested in East New York,
and we all clapped because he was still alive.
He told the story—stopped as a passenger
in a stolen car, which, of course, turned out
not to be stolen after all.
"Run so I can shoot you, nigger,"
a policeman said to Billy,
who shook and whirled inside
like a blender. He had to concentrate

on his feet, keep them steady
so there'd be no mistake about any sudden movements.
He was tossed in a cell, questioned
about the two hundred dollars in his front pocket
since he was on his way to buy his girlfriend
a ring for her birthday. The white cops
made fun of his musk oil, stepped on his sunglasses
though, he was assured later, this was by mistake.
Though everyone in America is still entitled
to that clichéd one call, this particular jail
in East New York didn't have a pay phone
that worked. Billy cried into his cot,
and the guard called him a mama's boy,
hitting him, heel of his palm to Billy's head.
No phone, they laughed the first 48 hours,
and the tri-state Dragnet team took two more days
after that to find him, even though
he was in one of their own jails.
Billy told us his story Thursday morning,
and to cut the tension I said he could have an extension
on his paper. He said not to worry,
he had a good lawyer from Jacoby and Meyers.
Those of the class who knew better groaned.
"You need a great lawyer," I said.
"An expert in civil suits—you could sue the city.
Just think of the psychological damages
to your family alone." Then someone in the back row
held up *The Post*, the front page declaring
the jury had acquitted
the policemen who'd beaten Rodney King.
We all knew what we had seen—
yet today's paper seemed less real,
more frightening than the videotape.
I wrote the words "irony" and "metaphor"
in big block letters on the chalkboard.
Billy stood up and bowed,
the best of definitions we could come up with.

Four Hours

My sister picks up her daughters at the bus stop
ever since a nine-year-old girl from the neighborhood
was coaxed into a car by a man
telling her he'd hit a kitten down the road.
His story went that the small ball of fur
ran somewhere near the railroad tracks
and he needed an extra pair of eyes to find it.
The girl was smart and had been taught
everything grown-ups thought she'd have to know
about even the worst of strangers, but she wanted
to be a veterinarian when she grew up.
And the man looked as though he'd been crying.
"He had that child in the car four hours,"
my mother tells me, my mother who would cut off his balls
if she had the chance. She sounds fed up, middle-class,
when she says it, and I want to say "no,"
but I too share her sentiment. My father
thinks the rapist deserves worse, to be shot dead—
no questions asked. My brother-in-law has a gun,
and my sister knows he'd use it if anyone tried to touch
their daughters, my nieces, my parents' grandchildren.
Four hours is longer than some double features,
longer than some continental plane rides,
longer than a whole afternoon in grade school.
Nothing is slower than time when you're nine years old,
nothing is more fragile than trust.
The rapist dropped the girl off at the pizza parlor
where the men who worked there called an ambulance.
Before this, my nieces walked the short distance home
and they protest, wanting to know why they can't anymore.
The after-school rapist hasn't been caught,
but the second and fifth grade rumors aren't terrifying enough.
My sister wonders how to tell her daughters,
who love small animals and only want to help.

David Lemieux

My first boyfriend is dead of AIDS. The one
who bought me a terrarium with a cactus
I watered until it became soft. The one

who took me to his junior high prom where I was shy
about dancing in public. The one who was mistaken
for a girl by a clerk when he wanted to try on a suit.

In seventh grade my first boyfriend and I looked a lot alike:
chubby arms, curly hair, our noses touching
when we tried our first kiss. My first boyfriend

was the only one who met my grandmother
before she died. Though, as a rule, she didn't like boys,
I think she liked my first boyfriend.

My first boyfriend and I sat in the backseat
of my mother's car, and on the ledge behind us
was a ceramic ballerina with a missing arm.

We were driving somewhere to have her repaired
or maybe to buy the right kind of glue.
My first boyfriend was rich and had horses

and airplanes he could fly by remote control.
My first boyfriend died on a mattress
thrown on the back of a pick-up

because the ambulance wouldn't come.
There was a garden in my first boyfriend's yard.
One day his mother said to us,

"Pick out some nice things for lunch."
My first boyfriend and I pulled at the carrot tops,
but all we came up with were little orange balls

that looked like kumquats without the bumps.
My first boyfriend and I heard ripping through the soil
that sounded close to our scalps, like a hair brush

through tangles. We were the ones who pushed
the tiny carrots back down, hoping they were able
to reconnect to the ground. We were the ones.

Fear on 11th Street and Avenue A, New York City

Now the papers are saying pesticides will kill us
rather than preservatives. I pass the school yard
where the Catholic girls snack. Cheeze Doodles and apples.
No parent today knows what to pack in a lunch box
and the plaid little uniforms
hold each girl in: lines in the weave cross
like directions, blurry decisions.
A supervising nun sinks in her wimple. All the things she can't do,
she thinks, to save them, her face growing smaller.
She dodges their basketball.
Who said the Catholic Church has you for life
if it had you when you were five? I remember my prayers at odd times
and these girls already look afraid.
But it's not just the church. It's America.
I fear the children I know will become missing children,
that I will lose everyone I need to some hideous cancer.
I fear automobiles, all kinds of relationships.
I fear that the IRS will find out the deductions I claimed this year
I made up, that an agent will find a crumpled draft of this poem
even if fear edits this line out. . . . I have no privacy,
no protection, yet I am anonymous. I sometimes think
the sidewalk will swallow me up. So I know when the girls
line up to go inside and one screams to her friend
"If you step on a crack, you'll break your mother's back. . . ."
she means it. She feels all that responsibility, that guilt.
There's only one brown girl who doesn't do what she should.
She's dancing by herself to a song on her Walkman.
One of her red knee socks bunches at her ankle and slips into her sneaker.
And the shoulder strap of her jumper has unbuckled so her bib flaps.
Maybe she can save us. I clutch the school yard's chain link fence.
Please, little girl, grow up to be pope or president.

For the One Man Who Likes My Thighs

There was the expensive cream from France
that promised the dimples would vanish
if applied nightly to the problem spots.
Then, when that didn't work, Kiko, the masseuse
at Profile Health Spa, dug her thumbs
deep into my flesh as she explained
in quasi-scientific terms that her rough hands
could break up the toughest globules of cellulite.
I screamed, then bruised over, but nothing
else happened. When they healed, my legs still looked
like tapioca pudding. There was the rolling pin method
I tried as far back as seventh grade,
kneading my lumpy legs as though I were making bread.
Cottage Cheese Knees, Thunder Thighs—
I heard it all—under the guise of teasing,
under the leaky umbrella mistaken for affection.
I learned to choose long dresses
and dark woolen tights, clam diggers instead of short-shorts,
and, when I could get away with it, skirted bathing suits.
The nutritionist said that maybe Royal Jelly tablets
would break up the fat. I drank eight glasses of water
every day for a month. I ate nothing
but steak for a week. I had to take everyone's advice,
fearing that if I didn't, my thighs
would truly be all my own fault. Liposuction
cost too much. The foil sweat-it-out
shorts advertised in the back of *Redbook*
didn't work. Swimming, walking in place, leg lifts.
It's embarrassing, especially being a feminist.
I wondered if Andrea Dworkin had stopped worrying,
and how. If Gloria Steinem does aerobics,
claiming it's just for her own enjoyment.
Then I read in a self-help book:
if you learn to appreciate your thighs, they'll appreciate
you back. Though it wasn't romance at first sight,
I did try to thank my legs for carrying me up nine flights

the day when the elevator at work was out;
for their quick sprint that propelled me
through the closing doors of the subway
so I wouldn't be late for a movie;
for supporting my nieces who straddled, one
on each thigh, their heads burrowing deep into my lap.
I think, in fact, that it was at that moment
of being an aunt I forgot for an instant
about my thigh dilemma and began, more fully,
as they say, enjoying my life. So when it happened later
that I fell in love, and as a bonus,
the man said he liked my thighs, I shouldn't have been
so thoroughly surprised. At first I was sure I'd misheard—
that he liked my eyes, that he had heard someone else sigh,
or maybe that he was having a craving for french fries.
And it wasn't very easy to nonchalantly say *oh, thanks*
after I'd made him repeat. I kept asking
if he was sure, then waiting for a punch
line of some mean-spirited thigh-related joke.
I ran my finger over his calf, brown and firm,
with beautiful muscles waving down the back.
It made no sense the way love makes no sense.
Then it made all the sense in the world.

The Woman with
Two Vaginas (1995)

A story is not true unless the storyteller puts something of his own in it.
—ANONYMOUS STORYTELLER FROM NAIN, LABRADOR

Him-Whose-Penis-Never-Slept

(a poem told in the style of an Inuit tale)

There was a husband who married a wife he found so beautiful
that his penis was in a state of constant arousal.
His wife was delicate and needed her sleep, but the needy penis
kept after her night and day. She served her husband dinner
and he wanted to have sex. Her shoulder brushed his as she passed
in the igloo's passageway and he wanted to have sex again. He often woke
      her up
in the middle of the night, his hard penis nudging against her thigh.
Soon he'd rubbed inside her so many times, that her vagina
wore away. The husband didn't see his mistake
and stroked his penis between her knees until his wife had no more legs.
He used up her belly and her arms. Her breasts were next
to disappear. When nothing was left that he could touch,
Him-Whose-Penis-Never-Slept ejaculated into his wife's shadow.
It vanished, his semen a liquid ghost dripping down a lonely snow wall.

The Hollow Men

(from the Inuit tale *The Entrails Thief*)

The land of Island Ice was forbidden,
yet three men journeyed there to hunt reindeer.
So plentiful were the animals, these men
built a little igloo and decided to stay for a visit.
As they were sleeping, the old spirit
Aukjuk, the stealer of entrails,
passed directly through their temporary ice wall.
Dish in hand, she walked up to the first man
and sucked out his entrails without waking him.
She emptied the second and third hunter
and left carrying her laden dish.
The men were so light now, they rose to the sky
and stopped at the moon. Even the powerful Moon Man
was no match for Aukjuk. He sent the hollow men
back to earth, to their wives
who had to tie their husbands
to their sleeping cots
so they wouldn't float away.

Vagina

(from the East Greenland Inuit tale *Utsuuq*)

One day a fisherman's penis got tangled up in his harpoon line.
The fisherman was never really good at catching seals
and as both prey and hunter tugged and hauled in opposite directions,
the man felt all the strength gush out of his penis.
He was relieved, if the truth be known.
He went home and dressed up like a woman.
He called himself Vagina and announced he was in need of a husband.
His mother was not happy about this.
She threatened to kick her son, who was now her daughter, out of the house
if he didn't again dress like a man and go out on the hunt.
Vagina knew a little magic, so she stripped the skin from her body
until she was just a skeleton. Her mother dropped dead in fright.
Vagina put her skin back on and started to behave
more and more like a woman. She fretted with her hair
and drew little tattoos all over her arms. Monthly
she made cuts at her groin so she could bleed.
She spent her days quietly softening fox skins with her teeth.
Vagina was still having trouble getting a husband
when a neighbor agreed to loan hers. When Vagina
removed her dress, the neighbor's husband
noticed her penis and called Vagina a madman.
Again, Vagina removed her skin as if to prove deep down
there was no difference between women and men
and their skeletons. Instead of consenting to have sex,
the man was so frightened he fell dead, like Vagina's mother, on the spot.
Vagina thought at least she could adopt
and then a child would provide her with company.
There was an orphan no one else would have.
Vagina tended to him like the kindest of mothers
until one day the boy demanded blubber.
"Can't you see I'm a woman?" Vagina said,
"I'm not allowed on the hunt. Find yourself a father,
a husband for me, and then we'll have plenty to eat."
The orphan was sharp. He had seen Vagina pissing
while standing up. He accused his mother of being a man.
Vagina, on impulse, became a skeleton again.
The orphan, instead of being scared, ran his fingers

over his mother's eyeball sockets and ribs. He drew a circle
around her pelvis and laughed. Vagina was forced
to use stronger magic. She reached into her chest
and pulled out her entrails. "There," she exclaimed,
"do you still insist on having some blubber?"
The orphan hugged his mother as some dogs
burst their way into the igloo, stealing, among other things, Vagina's intestines.
She shouted, "Stop!" and chased the dogs
for miles. But before she could catch up, the biggest dog had eaten her heart.
And everyone knows a person is nothing without that.
Slowly Vagina wasted away as the orphan watched.
The orphan buried his mother beneath a pile of stones,
loving her in spite of her magic and foolish penis.
Loving his dead mother in spite of her skeleton games,
the orphan went to search for seals and whales and blubber on his own.

The Raping of the Sun

(from the Inuit tale *Moon Rapes His Sister Sun*)

The dance house went dark
when a wind blew out all the lamps.
The singing continued in the blackness
while a boy raped a young girl.
He ran away just before the lamps
were relit, and the girl, crying,
made her way home on the crunchy snow.
She was a girl who loved to dance
and didn't want this pleasure taken from her,
so the next night she returned to the dance house
with soot on her hands, so that if this violence
happened again, she'd dirty
her attacker's back. After the second time—
the terrifying darkness, the pain, the rekindle—
the girl saw her palm prints on her brother's parka.
She cried, "Such things are unheard of!"
Her body still felt the ache of his presence
as she took a sharp knife and cut off both her breasts.
She flung them into his hands, screaming,
"You seem to have a taste for my body—Eat these!"
He held her bleeding breasts, in shock.
She grabbed a torch and fled the dance house.
No one is sure if the brother meant to apologize
or simply attack his sister again, when he followed,
stumbling and falling, snow putting out the flames
of his torch so that only its embers flickered.
A wind, more colossal than the one that disturbed
the dance hall lamps, lifted the man
and his breastless sister up high into the sky.
The girl became the sun who does all she can
to alleviate the dangers of the dark.
She stays as far away as possible
from her brother, the cold dim moon.

The Woman with Two Vaginas

(from the Baffin Island Inuit tale *Arnatsiq*)

The woman with two vaginas tried her best
to hide them from her husband. It was difficult
because her vaginas weren't in the usual place

but in the palms of her hands. To distract her husband,
she tickled his penis with her nipple,
or she took him into her backside.

She had traveled far, from a place she preferred
not to talk about, and her husband assumed
she learned her sexual practices there. He was happy

until he discovered his wife
pissing through her fingers, as though she were trying
to cup running water. He wished

that he didn't know what he then knew—
that his sexy young wife was also a ghost.
This was no time for sentimental lust—

a ghost can only bring loneliness to a snow hut.
So he strapped his wife into his kayak
and deposited her on an ice floe far from home.

He told her to go back to the Land of the Dead,
but she was trapped like a moving shadow
that was neither here nor there. Some say

they still hear her sobbing: "My husband
will not have me! My husband will not have me!"
But she has no way of knowing how he misses her

twin vaginas, how he tries his best to
hide it from his new wife—yet the village is small,
the gossip as fast as wind during a storm.

It's said he makes his new wife slap his face,
to feel the warm tingle of her fingers,
that he then cries out into her barren palms.

My Grandmother Is My Husband

(from the Inuit tale *Tuglik and Her Granddaughter*)

I was left alone with only grandmother,
as the youngest and oldest of our village, prohibited
from the narwhal hunt. No one came back
for years, not mother nor father, not the girls nor boys
who I imagine would by now kiss my cheeks
with snowballs, if they were still here.
Luckily for me, my grandmother was magic.
With a few words and a trance, she could turn herself
into a man. Her seal-bone penis
was always full of pleasure, her blubber-balls
were always warm. And being a man, she was able
to get food without as much danger. Her vagina
transformed into a mighty sled. She created
a team of dogs from her own lice. I spent my days
hidden in the hut, sewing animal skins and singing.
Grandmother always returned by evening,
sometimes with a ptarmigan, his dead feathered feet
stiff in the cold. I learned how to cook
all kinds of soup. This went on for many days of dark
and light, many years and changes in my body.
Sometimes I feared my handsome grandmother's death
and wondered if I'd be able to hunt for myself.
How could I sleep without her curled into me?
It came to pass that I would have other worries.
One day when I was alone a man came to our house.
His penis was real skin and blood. He showed me
his wrinkled testicles with pride. He wanted to know
whose harpoon stood in the corner. Whose kayak
leaned against the wall. Whose child filled my belly.
I told him they all belonged to my grandmother,
my husband. I kicked as he threw me over his shoulder,
promising he would make me a happier wife.
Grandmother returned that evening as usual,
a walrus roped onto her sled. She cried out my name
over and over, looking for boiling water, some proof
that I was coming back. She saw no point

in hunting or eating anything else. She saw no point
in being a man any more. She undid
her magic spell—man or woman, it's all the same
when a person dies alone.

Girl Soldier (1996)

When I Was a Lesbian

I went out with a woman
more macho than any of my boyfriends.
Jo was into fisting, a rack
of ties in her closet
of wool suits, boxer shorts
under her black jeans.
If that didn't prove she was man enough,
she loved to tell of the time she'd stabbed someone
before she stopped shooting up.
Her one regret—crack wasn't around
before she went straight.
I thought I could relate—
I'd given up sugar
before Pepperidge Farm invented
those huge soft Nantuckets.
We both still craved something,
something other than each other.
I had to compete with Bunny,
her mistress who stripped
in a club in Times Square.
Nothing was the way I pictured my life
as a dyke—two soft women in granny skirts
holding hands. Where were the herbal teas,
the Holly Near concerts, the tarot card readings?
Jo rarely said anything nice to me.
When I broke it off, all she could pout:
"Please don't go. You have nice breasts."
Her woman's throat, deep with regret.
She threatened to come after me if I wrote
about any of this. So I've changed her name
to Jo from Sid. I won't say what city
she lives in. Sometimes I think I gave up
too fast, that Jo was wrong—I wasn't a scorned hetero
fed up with men. I was just a Ben
Franklin, my kite in the air
night after rainy night, then
sick in bed with a head cold
the one time lightning was meant to strike.

Making Money

It was Gertrude Stein who said
she loved cold hard cash, but hated
doing any of the things she had to do
to get it. Consider phone sex,
what it would be like for a woman
who has been raped twice
to whisper "Ooh baby, ooh,"
into a mouthpiece to a man
who'd like to squeeze her wrists
until they bruise. Consider teaching
freshman composition at a community college,
piles of notebook-fringed papers
on your coffee table. After a while,
getting mixed up yourself
by the subjunctive for conjectures,
the proper use of was and were. The donut shop
is hiring, where you've worked before.
The sweet smell of lard and sugar
cooked into your skin. You could send away
for a kit and become a television repairman.
You could stuff envelopes, a penny apiece,
in the privacy of your own home.
Or dig out your pink-collar waitress uniform,
the cashier's smock, or the factory apron.
Why didn't you ever study accounting?
You could get your other old job back at the shoe store.
You've already tried being a journalist,
but could never really stick to the facts:
describing the tragic car wreck as *cold metal death*.
When you switched to just entering data,
the computer screen made your eyes water.
When you were a candy striper,
you went home and cried
as though you knew the dying boy
personally. And that was only volunteer.
So I guess being a doctor is out.
Your mother is a nurse,

and so you'd have no white-dress fantasies,
she told you early what it was really like.
Covering for the doctor's mistakes,
emptying out bedpans. Have you heard
about the latest scam, making money
in your spare time, as you sleep?
The *Assyrian Dream Book* claims
images of eating feces will bring wealth.
No prior experience required, but lucid dreaming is a plus.

From the Shore

Michele and I pull out our feet from the mud, and begin
to scream from a new spot. We think you are going to drown.
You won't look back as you swim to the middle of the ocean.

"But Ma!" We call. Chills through our arms, down
through our legs as though we've been struck still by lightning
and no one will touch us. We're afraid to touch each other.

If only we could jump out past our bodies, the small ones
you had to lift up when the waves came. Michele and I clung
to your sides and still got mouthfuls of saltwater.

Had we dragged mud from the sand castle to the blanket
or sung too loud or fought with each other? The foam
like thrown toys breaking at our feet, unsteadying us.

At sunset, the family beach mostly cleared,
a lady with red veins on her legs and a bathing suit with a skirt
stops to help us. We point you out, the only mother

in the lineup. Your face, a small craft at the point where water
meets choppy sky. The lady says it's about to rain
and starts yelling with us, demanding you get back on shore

to take care of your daughters. I know we've made a mistake
as you turn around and see Michele and me with this other adult.
All the ocean goes silent—the sea sounds, the gulls.

It's like watching TV with the sound turned off.
You rise from the water like a wet monster and the lady,
in a rage, begins to yell and I guess you yell back:

my ears are murmuring a quiet that's louder.
I vow never to tell on anyone again—if ever I see a kid hitting
another kid, if ever I see someone robbing a bank.

My whole body shakes, the sound inside a seashell.
You yank Michele's arm and mine, saying,
"Can't I have one Goddamn minute alone?"

How to Help Children through Wartime

(January 24, 1991)

Mister Rogers says to tell your American young
it's OK to be sad. Present them a globe
rather than a flat map to show-and-tell
how far away the Middle East really is. Stress
that the TV Saudi weather report
doesn't mean the country is within driving distance. Stress
that their U.S. president assures them all life is precious,
an Iraqi child's equal to that of an American soldier.
Tell your children this, whether or not
you yourself believe him. Tell children that parents,
be they civilian or soldier, love them regardless
of what soil they're on. Consider letting children know
what the war is really like,
but if your daughter has Nintendo, do not pour blood
instead of milk on her Cheerios. If your son
is in a dangerous gang, let him explain
war to you instead. Encourage all elementary schoolers
to take their chemistry sets to the sandbox.
If you teach art, explain current events
with paper dolls. A strand of red construction paper men:
George Bush, Dick Cheney, Saddam Hussein, et cetera.
Have students crumble up one doll and name him
Noriega. They may throw him in a Dixie cup
that represents a jail. Then, you may ask questions
that lead students to notice the resemblance
of one paper man to the next. Have each of the children
pick a doll who represents their favorite.
Instruct them to cut that man up into the teeniest pieces
their safety paper scissors will permit.
Members of the class may begin to get restless, to sprinkle
each other with the crimson bits. Allow this:
confetti, bloodshed, red snow, bombs.

Summer

My mother's wet feet left paw prints on the deck,
her arches fallen like a bear's.
She sat in her polar white bathing suit,
her calves dangling in the pool.
Once we were sure she'd eaten our father
when he didn't come home from work.
Her hands pounced at the innocent air
as a bee circled her hairsprayed chignon.
Then she slept in the lounge chair all afternoon.

Whole

I learned to masturbate late,
in my mid-twenties, with a self-help book
in my loft bed in the East Village.
A few blocks over at an underground club
people were having orgasms in public,
and on stage at the Pyramid,
Annie Sprinkle showed her cervix
to all who were interested. As I learned to dance
around the primal scream that was my clitoris,
around the pink cartoon blurb missing words,
I was in kindergarten gym again. Mr. Lynn
held his left open hand against my back
and his right open hand under the wing span
of my ribs. The forest green mat before me
was spooky, everything dark
beyond my small town. When I tried to explain
I'd never done a tumble before,
he grew impatient, his hands somehow unbuckling
my taut legs until I was kneeling at the edge
of that plastic forest that smelled of sweat. I was sure
I'd break my neck, that my head
would be crushed under the weight of my stiff back.
I half-abandoned myself to death
when I heard the girls behind me, waiting their turns,
sizzle with impatient whispers. My rolling was far from perfect,
the almost-horizontal lost hubcap seconds before its collapse.
I think a few children laughed, my body sideways,
my legs off the mat. And everyone else went on,
perfectly whole as bagels, donuts, and bicycle wheels.
Some even lined up to do it again and again.

Feminism

All over the world, Little Bees, Star Scouts,
and Blue Birds play Telephone, whispering messages
in a chain link of ears—no repeating (that's cheating),
only relaying what they hear their first shot.
Sometimes "Molly loves Billy" becomes "A Holiday in Fiji,"
or "Do the Right Thing" becomes "The Man Who Would Be King."
Still, there is trust. Girls taking the Blind Walk,
a bandana around one's eyes (Pin the Tail on the Donkey–style)
as another leads her through the woods
or a backyard or entire city blocks. Girls helping
where they are needed or inventing ways to aid
where they seemingly are not. Memorizing remedies
for cuts and stings, frostbite, nosebleeds.
Their motto: Be prepared at all times.
Full of anxiety, they watch for home hazards,
check for frayed toaster or hair dryer cords.
Outside they watch for color changes in cloud formations,
the darkening of the sky. They're safest in cars
during electrical storms.
                              There's so much to remember and learn.
So many impending disasters, yet so many well-wishes
for their world. These girls shut the tap
as they brush their teeth, secure glow-in-the-dark reflectors
on their bikes, and do at least one good turn daily.
They are taught that alone they are small,
but if they can empathize with each other, they can gain power.
Just to see what it feels like, a walking girl
may spend an afternoon in a wheelchair. Another
may stuff cotton in her ears. And to be readied
for what lies ahead when they grow up
and they're no longer Girl Scouts, they make collages
cutting images from magazines showing what they might be:
mothers or lawyers, reporters or nurses.
Or they play Rabbit without a House, a Brazilian form
of London Bridge, or American Musical Chairs.
There will always be an odd number of girls, always
one left out. The earth and her scarce resources.
Survival in Sudan begins with Sheep And Hyena.

And though the girls may try to protect the one
who is the Sheep in the middle of their circle, most often
the outside Hyena does not give up
and breaks through sore forearms and weakened wrists
to eat her. Red Rover, Red Rover,
it is better when Girl Scouts stay together.
So they bond tightly in their Human Knot,
a female version of the football team's huddle.
And all holding hands, they squeeze their Friendship Squeeze,
knowing each small one-at-a-time grip
is like a Christmas tree light, each a twinkle
the rest of the strand cannot do without.
Each missing face on the missing child poster
like the fairest of all looking into her mirror.

How the Sky Fell
(1996)

How the Sky Fell

"Chicken Licken told Henny Penny who told Drake Lake who told Duck Luck who told Loose Goose. . . ."

Some said it was just an acorn. Others, a teeny meteorite
or a pebble thrown from the highway above Chicken Licken.
Her friends thought she was overreacting—
Her car had been stolen twice this year. Her purse
had been torn from her shoulder by kids at the mall.
And all this on top of a nasty custody battle.
Surely, it must have felt like her world was crashing in.
"The sky is falling," Chicken Licken told her ex-husband Cheater Peter
who told his lawyer Glib Fib who told the jury, the Delve Twelve,
who told the media, Whose News.
The talk show hosts, the Tantalize Guys, asked Chicken Licken
to come onto their programs and tell the whole world about the faulty sky.
The housewives Home Joans and the kids Wee Latch Keys
giggled at Chicken Licken's hysterical TV plea.
Her own children, Howl Fowl and Nerd Bird,
knew it was all over as their mother made her apocalyptic
televised warnings. The children would be stuck living
with Cheater Peter and his new girlfriend Spacey Stacie
from now on. Everyone ignored the few call-ins,
the Phone Clones, who agreed with Chicken Licken,
who had similar sky-nuggets crash onto them. For the most part,
Chicken Licken preached to an empty congregation
as nature's rafters gave way under heaven's weight,
as the clothespins that held up her sky rotted away.

Blue Beard's One-Hundredth Wife

This was before battered women's shelters,
before serial killers were called serial killers,
before divorce, even before handguns.
Blue Beard's one-hundredth wife found his dead ninety-nine others
stored in a forbidden room. Some said he tired of a woman
once her mystery faded. Others thought
he was too quick to temper. He went on
long business trips before there were business trips,
trying perhaps to curb his domestic violence.
His beard was blue before punk rock was fashionable,
which manipulated some women into feeling bad for him.
They stroked his speckled mustache—his navy bristles
and his soft gray hairs, which grew in aqua.
He curled into their breasts, playing sensitive,
his big rough hands stroking the backs of their necks.
In a week or two a wedding, in another month
she'd drop a dish or smell up the outhouse
and it was all over. No one ever found his weapon.
Certain forensics specialists guessed he used his bare hands,
pulling his wives apart as though they were roasted chickens.
Luckily for them, this was before magic was obsolete
and Blue Beard's one-hundredth wife knew how to sew.
When she found that pile of dead wife parts
she pieced them together like Butterick patterns
and took to arms and heads with a needle and thread.
After two afternoons of nonstop work,
the women breathed again, all perfectly proportioned.
Some said, "Thank you, I've always wanted red hair."
Or, "Wow! I wondered what it was like to have big breasts!"
Blue Beard's one-hundredth wife sewed the light eyes
to the light skin, the small ankles on the small legs.
This was before plastic surgery, this was before women's magazines,
before body doubles were used in movies. Yet here were ninety-nine
untouchable pinups, their creator a Plain Jane
with a good eye for detail. When Blue Beard came home
his grief shook the stained glass windows of his castle.
He tried to kill his one-hundredth wife,

using the excuse of her entrance into the forbidden room,
but his ninety-nine exes pushed him out his heavy oak front door.
This was before lawyers, but the one hundred wives still got the house.

The Ugly Stepsister

You don't know what it was like.
My mother marries this bum who takes off on us,
after only a few months, leaving his little Cinderella
behind. Oh yes, Cindy will try to tell you
that her father died. She's like that, she's a martyr.
But between you and me, he took up
with a dame close to Cindy's age.
My mother never got a cent out of him
for child support. So that explains
why sometimes the old lady was gruff.
My sisters and I didn't mind Cindy at first,
but her relentless cheeriness soon took its toll.
She dragged the dirty clothes to one of Chelsea's
many laundromats. She was fond of talking
to mice and rats on the way. She loved doing dishes
and scrubbing walls, taking phone messages,
and cleaning toilet bowls. You know,
the kind of woman that makes the rest
of us look bad. My sisters and I
weren't paranoid, but we couldn't help
but see this manic love for housework
as part of Cindy's sinister plan. Our dates
would come to pick us up and Cindy'd pop out
of the kitchen offering warm chocolate chip cookies.
Critics often point to the fact that my sisters and I
were dark and she was blonde, implying
jealousy on our part. But let me
set the record straight. We have the empty bottles
of Clairol's Nice 'n Easy to prove
Cindy was a fake. She was what her shrink called
a master manipulator. She loved people
to feel bad for her—her favorite phrase was a faint,
"I don't mind. That's OK." We should have known
she'd marry Jeff Charming, the guy from our high school
who went on to trade bonds. Cindy finagled her way
into a private Christmas party on Wall Street,
charging a little black dress at Barney's,

which she would have returned the next day
if Jeff hadn't fallen head over heels.
She claimed he took her on a horse-and-buggy ride
through Central Park, that it was the most romantic
evening of her life, even though she was home
before midnight—a bit early, if you ask me, for Manhattan.
It turned out that Jeff was seeing someone else
and had to cover his tracks. But Cindy didn't
let little things like another woman's happiness
get in her way. She filled her glass slipper
with champagne she had lifted
from the Wall Street extravaganza. She toasted
to Mr. Charming's coming around, which he did
soon enough. At the wedding, some of Cindy's friends
looked at my sisters and me with pity. The bride insisted
that our bridesmaids' dresses should be pumpkin,
which is a hard enough color for anyone to carry off.
But let me assure you, we're all very happy
now that Cindy's moved uptown. We've
started a mail order business—cosmetics
and perfumes. Just between you and me,
there's quite a few bucks to be made
on women's self-doubts. And though
we don't like to gloat, we hear Cindy Charming
isn't doing her aerobics anymore. It's rumored
that she yells at the maid, then locks herself in her room,
pressing hot match tips into her palm.

Kinky (1997)

One Afternoon when Barbie Wanted to Join the Military

It was a crazy idea, she admits now,
but camouflage was one costume she still hadn't tried.
Barbie'd gone mod with go-go boots during Vietnam.
Throughout Panama she was busy playing with a Frisbee
the size of a Coke bottle cap. And while troops
were fighting in the Gulf,
she wore a gown inspired by Ivana Trump.
When Mattel told her, hell no—she couldn't go,
Barbie borrowed GI Joe's fatigues,
safety pinning his pants's big waist
to better fit her own.
She settled on his olive tank.
But Barbie thought it was boring.
"Why don't you try running over something small?"
coaxed GI Joe, who sat naked behind the leg
of a human's living room chair.
Barbie saw imaginary bunnies
hopping through the shag carpet.
"I can't," she said.
GI Joe suggested she gun down the enemy,
who was sneaking up behind her.
Barbie couldn't muster up the rage
for killing, even if it was only play.
Maybe if someone tried to take her parking space
or scratched her red Trans Am.
Maybe if someone had called her a derogatory name.
But what had this soldier from the other side done?
GI Joe, seeing their plan was a mistake,
asked her to return his clothes,
making Barbie promise not to tell anyone.
As she slipped back into her classic baby blue
one-piece swimsuit, she realized
this would be her second secret.
She couldn't tell about the time
she posed nude for *Hustler*.
A young photographer who lived in the house
dipped her legs in a full bottle of Johnson's Baby Oil,
then swabbed some more on her torso.

Barbie lounged on the red satin lining
of the kid's Sunday jacket. He dimmed
the lights and lit a candle
to create a glossy centerfold mood.
"Lick your lips," he kept saying,
forgetting Barbie didn't have a tongue.
She couldn't pout. She couldn't even bite
the maraschino cherry he dangled in front of her mouth.
Luckily there was no film in his sister's camera,
so the boy's pictures never came out.
Luckily GI Joe wasn't in the real Army
or he said he would risk being court-martialed—
he wasn't supposed to lend his uniform
to anyone, especially a girl.
Just then a human hand deposited Ken from the sky.
Somewhere along the way he'd lost his sandals.
"What have you two been up to?" he asked.
Barbie didn't have the kind of eyes that could shift away
so she lost herself in the memory of a joke
made by her favorite comedian Sandra Bernhard,
who said she liked her dates to be androgynous
because if she was going to be with a man
she didn't want to have to face that fact.
Barbie was grateful for Ken's plastic flat feet
and plastic flat crotch. No military
would ever take him, even if there was a draft.
As GI Joe bullied Ken into a headlock,
Barbie told the boys to cut it out. She threatened
that if he kept it up, GI Joe would
never get that honorable discharge.

Bisexual Barbie

One of ten Barbies is left-handed,
another ten percent are lesbian.
But it's hard to keep track of the bisexual ones—
their orientation often secret, or if overt,
still undetectable. Barbies dress in front of one another
and statisticians think nothing of it.
Two Barbies often share a sleeping bag or double bed
because there are twice as many Barbies as Kens.
Two Barbies live in one Furnished Glamour Home
when each could easily afford her own.
When a Barbie closes her eyes, it's hard for her to tell
if she is reaching out to another Barbie or a Ken.
Female or male, the plastic doll-skin
is equally cool and smooth. Bald seamless crotches,
equally dry and unresponsive to touch. Both
have hard chests and legs that resist being spread.
The giveaway is always the hair, Ken's
simply a splash of paint over his scalp.
But how many lonely Barbies—who've taken sophisticated trips
to Greece, New York City, and Italy—can be so straight
as to let a blond ponytail get in their way?

Oriental Barbie

She could be from Japan, Hong Kong, China,
the Philippines, Vietnam, Thailand, or Korea.
The little girl who plays with her can decide.
The south, the north, a nebulous
province. It's all the same, according to Mattel, who says
this Barbie still has "round eyes,"
but "a smaller mouth and a smaller bust"
than her U.S. sister. Girls, like some grown men,
like variety, as long as it's pretty, as long
as there's long hair to play with.
On a late-night Manhattan Cable commercial,
one escort service sells *Geishas to Go,*
girls from "the Orient, where men are kings. . . ."
White Ken lies on his stomach
while an Oriental Barbie walks on his back.
Or is it a real woman stepping on Ken?
Or Oriental Barbie stepping on a real man?
You have to travel to Japan
to buy this particular Barbie doll. A geisha girl
can be at the door of your New York apartment
in less than an hour. Of course,
there is no Oriental Ken.
Those who study the delicate balance
of American commerce and trade understand.

Kinky

They decide to exchange heads.
Barbie squeezes the small opening under her chin
over Ken's bulging neck socket. His wide jawline jostles
atop his girlfriend's body, loosely,
like one of those nodding novelty dogs
destined to gaze from the back windows of cars.
The two dolls chase each other around the orange Country Camper,
unsure what they'll do when they're within touching distance.
Ken wants to feel Barbie's toes between his lips,
take off one of her legs and force his whole arm inside her.
With only the vaguest suggestion of genitals,
all the alluring qualities they possess as fashion dolls,
up until now, have done neither of them much good.
But suddenly Barbie is excited looking at her own body
under the weight of Ken's face. He is part circus freak,
part thwarted hermaphrodite. And she is imagining
she is somebody else—maybe somebody middle class and ordinary,
maybe another teenage model being caught in a scandal.

The night had begun with Barbie getting angry
at finding Ken's blow-up doll, folded and stuffed
under the couch. He was defensive and ashamed, especially about
not having the breath to inflate her. But after a round
of pretend-tears, Barbie and Ken vowed to try
to make their relationship work. With their good memories
as sustaining as good food, they listened to late-night radio
talk shows, one featuring Doctor Ruth. *When all else fails,
just hold each other,* the small sex therapist crooned.
Barbie and Ken, on cue, groped in the dark,
their interchangeable skin glowing, the color of Band-Aids.
Then, they let themselves go—Soon Barbie was begging Ken
to try on her spandex miniskirt. She showed him how
to pivot as though he were on a runway. Ken begged
to tie Barbie onto his yellow surfboard and spin her
on the kitchen table until she grew dizzy. *Anything,
anything,* they both said to the other's requests,
their mirrored desires bubbling from the most unlikely places.

Barbie's GYN Appointment

Her high arches defy the stirrups
and her legs refuse to open wide.
She has no complaints, cramps,
spottings, or flashes. It doesn't hurt
when the doctor presses on her abdomen.
There's nowhere for him to take a pap smear,
but Barbie's gynecologist suggests a D and C,
a hysterectomy, then a biopsy, just to be sure.
Barbie rebels as her breasts refuse to give
under the weight of the mammogram machine's plate.
She doesn't own a nightie suitable
for hospital wear, she explains, as she refuses operations
and scrunches the disposable examining frock
into a ball. She tosses it into the trash can
with relief. Not even Barbie looks good
in that pale green. She'll skip her follow-up appointment
on behalf of the rest of us who can't
and circle the globe, a tiny copy of *The New Our Bodies,*
Ourselves under her arm. The book will fire her imagination,
each chapter a fashion doll's version of the best science fiction.

Marriage

Barbie wonders if it's cheating
when she dreams of fashion doll boyfriends
Mattel never made for her to play with.
One with rastafarian dreadlocks—
spun with fuzz, not stiff
like the arcs of a plastic jello mold.
Another chubby and balding
with John Lennon glasses.
And a third with a big sexy nose
like Gerard Depardieu.
Still, she supposes, Ken is harmless enough.
His pecs kept at bay by her stiff unyielding breasts.
And there's nothing he can force on her
when she's not in the mood.
She remembers discontinued Midge's last words:
"Hey, Barbie, it's a marriage, don't knock it."
From the stack of boys' toys across the aisle,
GI Joe occasionally gives Barbie the eye,
though he's not exactly what she has in mind.
In her box, elastic bands hold back her arms
and the plastic overlay she peers through
distorts her view of the world.
It's not only a romantic fling she desires:
there are hot air balloon rides,
night school classes, charity work.
Barbie comforts herself
knowing she's not much different
from the rest of us, juggling gratitude,
ambition, passivity, and guilt.

Barbie Joins a Twelve Step Program

Barbie is *bottoming out,*
she's sitting on the *pity pot.* She hasn't the know-how to express
any of her emotions. Before she even gets
to her first meeting, she takes the first step, admits
her life has *become unmanageable.*
She's been kidnapped by boys
and tortured with pins. She's been left
for months at a time between scratchy couch cushions
with cracker crumbs, pens, and loose change.
She can't help herself from being a fashion doll.
She is the ultimate victim.

She humbly sits on a folding chair
in a damp church basement. The cigarette smoke
clouds the faces around her, the smell of bad coffee
permeates the air. The group booms the serenity prayer:
God, grant me serenity to accept the things I cannot change,
courage to change the things I can, and wisdom
to know the difference. Poor Barbie is lost
in a philosophical quandary. Her God must be Mattel.
How can she *turn her life and will over* to a toy company?
Must she accept her primary form of locomotion
being the fists of young careless humans?

And what can she change? The only reason Barbie
is at the meeting at all is because she wound up in the tote bag
of a busy mother. She toppled out when the woman,
putting on lipstick at the bathroom mirror, spilled the contents
of her bag onto the floor. The mother didn't see Barbie skid under a stall door
where a confused drunk, at the meeting for warmth,
was peeing. *Never thought Barbie had problems,*
she said, picking up the doll. She thought it would be funny
to prop Barbie in the last row. No one else noticed the doll
as she fidgeted in her seat. The hungry drunk
went on to spoon a cupful of sugar into her coffee.

Barbie sat through the meeting, wondering:
What is wisdom? What is letting go?
She wished she could clap like the others
when there was a good story about recovery. She accepted
she couldn't, hoping that if she stopped struggling,
her higher power, Mattel, would finally let her move.
Miracles don't happen overnight, said a speaker.
Take the action and leave the rest to God, said another.
Barbie's prayer that she would be at the next meeting was answered.
A member of the clean-up committee squished her between the seat
and back of the folding chair and stacked her, with the others, against the wall.

Barbie as Religious Fanatic

Eve, being one of the first born
ever, had no bellybutton because she'd sprung
from no womb. Barbie thinks how her birth, too,
was sterile and bloodless. Aligning herself with the holy,
she says proudly, *I will never miss the comfort of a uterus.*
I will never know a faulty mother.
But raised in a society that does its best
to trample female spirit, Barbie had also been taught
to feel bad about what she lacked. As hollow
as the Tin Man, she was ashamed
about her absent heart. She thought herself inadequate,
emptied of bones or bowels. So it was also the unfulfilled nature
of this doll that readied her for religion. Before the fall,
Eve, like Barbie, had no period, no cramps, no pain
in childbirth. And now Barbie's friend Judy,
The Mommy-to-Be Doll, similarly makes delivery a snap.
No stretch marks or screaming, no afterbirth or drugs.
Judy's stomach is a trap door that hides a clean infant
with a full head of hair. Take out the child, press her belly down,
and Judy can immediately fit into Barbie's clothes.
Barbie wonders if her friend is a sign:
Could Judy be a virgin though she has no vagina?
Could the immaculate conception be applied to plastic?
These tiny child-saviors, both White and Afro-American
like their mothers, could easily fit in the cribs
of decorative mangers in holiday homes.
Could the world's next messiah be a girl?
Could Barbie's friend Judy be the next Mary?
Although no biblical scholar,
Barbie is smart enough to put two and two together.
She knows she arrived years before Ken, without the help
of any of his ribs, which makes her wonder
about Adam, if he really did beat Eve
to the Garden of Eden. Barbie pictures herself, an apostle
to the initial wave of the second coming
as she collects her religious pamphlets—
the *Good News, Smile—God Loves You*, the ones
given out by the Jehovah's Witnesses. She crosses out

what she doesn't believe and sprinkles the text
with arrows and Judy's name. Shoppers gather
as Barbie preaches her version of religion at the corner
of the Toys-R-Us doll aisle. The wars
and natural disasters go on, surely, just
as Barbie predicts. Though the smaller children believe her,
at first they are too busy playing
to see her connections. Some heathen kids toss
Judy's baby daughter in the bottoms of their toy chests
to leave her there for years. Barbie says, *Doesn't anybody see?*
She puts on her bikini and points to where her bellybutton should be.
Her voice is sheer will, without the aid of battery
or pull string. And Mattel, Barbie claims, is her loving God.
She's especially successful in the conversion of girls
as they grow older and see their flaws. They praise
Barbie's paradise—her clothes, her homes, her cars.
She's as free as they ever hope to be—
with no toy-apples anywhere in sight.

Literary Barbie

When Barbie reads Kafka's *The Metamorphosis*,
her whole body aches. She relates
to Gregor Samsa, the salesman-turned-bug,
who tries to explain his transformation
to his family, but who can only
produce tiny insect-squeaks. So many times
that kind of thing has happened to her.
Barbie's ouches gone unacknowledged, silent giggles
indicating appreciated tickles, lost shrill cries
for help. From the other room, she overhears a human
telling her friend that women make Barbie-feet
just before orgasm, pointing their bare toes to the edge
of the bed, even though they aren't wearing high heels.
Barbie has a thought, unsure whether it is
memory or pure imagination:
                                    it's her, but not her,
under the stars, in a field of wet grass. She looks
like someone she doesn't know—a chubby girl
with problem skin and thick glasses. There is a hand,
her own or someone else's, between her legs
and she feels the beginnings of something
she's never felt before. In her terror of pleasure,
she whispers *no* to it all. And wakes up, immobile,
plastic, looking entirely like somebody else.

The Limited Edition Platinum Barbie

Ever since Marilyn Monroe
bleached her hair so it would photograph better
under the lights, Bob Mackie
wanted to do the same for Barbie.
Now here she is, a real fashion illustration,
finally a model whose legs truly make up
more than half her height. The gown is white,
and the hair more silver than Christmas,
swept up in a high pouf of intricate twists.
Less demanding than Diana Ross
or Cher, Barbie has fewer flaws to hide.
No plastic surgery scars, no
temper tantrums when Mackie's bugle beads
don't hang just right. Calvin Klein
won't design certain styles
for any women larger than size eight.
He "doesn't do upholstery," is the way
he likes to put it. So imagine Bob Mackie's thrill
of picking up this wisp of a model,
Barbie weighing less than a quart of milk.
Imagine him dressing her himself.
The eight thousand hand-sewn sequins,
which would have easily been eight million
if he had to design this gown for a bulky human.
Yes, Barbie is his favorite client—poised,
ladylike, complying. As he impales her
on her plastic display stand, Mackie's confident
she won't ruin any effect by bad posture.
Collectors can pay in four monthly installments
of $38.50 and have Barbie delivered to their home.
Others can go to Mackie's display at FAO Schwarz,
the most expensive toy store in New York,
to remind themselves of who they'll never be,
of what they'll never have.

The Star-Spangled Banner (1999)

June 13, 1995

The best place to turn thirty-four is in Mojácar, Spain,
where the women all have fine lines on their faces
from the constant sun, which stays out long enough
to kiss the moon that fades in the day but never really goes away,
hovering just above the mountains—in Mojácar, Spain,
where it is still sexy to have a tan and hips.
The houses here are all white and challenge the sun
to a boxing match of awe and brightness
so that sometimes the white turns blue from the sea
or green from the mountains or blond from the desert.
The houses are built into the sides of mountains
like teeth into gums and stand just as secure. And the hens
sing, really sing, and hold their notes better than a beginning choir.
And the sand leading to the Mediterranean is chocolate
at one end of the beach and pure sugar at the other.
And the Gypsy gives the evil eye to her client
who's gone to someone else for help because her first spell didn't work.
And there is no irony in spells or the Catholic Church,
the bells tolling from the pueblo to wake everyone up,
then reminding them at night to say their prayers.
And the women pull up their skirts, their calves in the public fountain,
and wash their clothes by hand and rub their panties and pillow cases
until the suds multiply like bubble bath, then the women carry away
jugs of water on their heads, quick and graceful as ants.
There is only the occasional satellite dish so Spaniards can laugh
at the absurdity of the O.J. Simpson trial or remark how handsome
O.J. is. Or say, *Poor Nicole, we have that too you know,*
the battering of wives, in our country. In the backyard
of the house where I'm staying, the archaeologist
finds a five-thousand-year-old skull
of a small girl in what looks to be a domicile—unless, he says,
it was some kind of sacrificial altar. The dig site
is as big as a Hollywood swimming pool, full of ancient tools
and animal jaw bones. I say to someone:
Nicole Brown Simpson has been dead a year already,
she was killed last year on my birthday.
The best place to turn thirty-four is in Mojácar, Spain,

where an archaeologist will cradle that girl-child's skull
in his arms for a minute before he dusts her off
and measures her eye sockets, as if he's truly sorry about what happened
all those decades and centuries and cruelties ago.

Cockroaches

That's what my father-in-law calls the American kids
who scamper through Europe each summer
with their backpacks and Eurail passes, some of them
even honeymooning, he says, disgusted. Such a small wardrobe,
such unattractive luggage. I don't tell him that I was a cockroach
fifteen Junes ago, making 300 American dollars last a whole month,
eating *arroz con pollo* four nights in a row in the cheapest restaurant
in Barcelona, that I washed my underwear in *pension* sinks.
I can't tell him these things because he is old
and elegant, embarrasses easily, knows about tax

shelters and deutsche marks and yen. Besides, he shares
what he has with me. O.K. It's true—technically
cockroaches are most active in summer months, but some believe
they can also cure skin ulcers when ground and mixed with sugar.
Scientists have just invented tiny video cameras
they can strap onto roaches who crawl through earthquake debris
and enemy hotel rooms, unnoticed, the perfect rescue workers and spies.
They were here on earth before we were; they'll likely
survive a nuclear attack. Most often cockroaches die on their backs.
I know this from the ones I lived with in New York City tenements.

You can kill roaches with mashed potatoes laced with arsenic,
or with black plastic discs full of poison. I hated them even before
I saw my first one. Roaches—that's what we called the boys next door
whose last name was Rochelle, whose father was a circus clown
with a bad temper when his make-up was off, whose above-the-ground
pool perched in their driveway—the dirty water, pea soup
thickened with a ham hock. "*La cucaracha, la cucaracha*,"
my sister and I sang as the younger brother peed
into their cat's litter box. Then he'd chase after us, trying
to pee on our new red Keds. My mother said,

"Keep away from those kids. They're full of lice
and trashy ideas." So how I saw the Rochelles was how
my husband's father would have seen me then: poking my tongue
through my missing front tooth, wearing a hand-me-down tee shirt
from my cousin that read "Sock it to me, baby,"

a phrase that had peaked in popularity a few years before.
My father and mother passing each other every day at three,
one working first, the other second shift. Hamburger Helper
and Coolwhip. We were cockroaches, happy as all the rest,
scurrying fast across the dirty tub we knew as America.

How Much Is This Poem Going to Cost Me?

It's not something I like to burden my readers with as a rule,
the process of spending money for paper and paper clips, pens,
ink cartridges for the printer—never mind the computer itself,
which is a whole other story.
                         My favorite uncle
was watching Phil Donahue—the topic was computers I guess—
and a journalist on the panel said, "No writer today
can live without one." My uncle called before the show was over
and offered to buy me my first computer. I dyed my hair red
for the first time, just days before he died. Some readers might think
that might be developed as a separate poem of its own, but since we're all
on tight budgets, I'll try to fit it in here:
                                    How I called all night
and he wouldn't answer his phone. How my sister found him
early the next morning. The tension over his will.
How my mother picked me up at the train station for the funeral,
crying into my shoulder—her dead older brother
who brought her a hula skirt from the South Pacific after the war,
who gave her away at her wedding since their father
had already passed on—before she suddenly got a grip on herself and said:
"What the hell have you done to your hair?" My mother hates redheads
for some reason, always saying she would have drowned her kids
if any of them had been born strawberry blonde or auburn.
When I was little, my uncle used to live in the apartment downstairs.
That was before his wife died, very young,
so they never had a chance to have kids. He told me he felt helpless;
it was like watching a dying little bird. . . .
                                    I pay for this poem in many ways.
Right now, as I write this, I could be at a job earning money
or, at the very least, looking at the help-wanted ads. I could be writing
a screenplay, a novel that would maybe, just maybe, in the end pay for itself.
Sure "there are worse things I could do" as the slutty girl
sings in *Grease*, although it's not politically correct to call her that.
What do people say nowadays? Sexually daring?
I've always liked that character Rizzo—the way she finds out
she's not pregnant after all at the end of the movie,

calling her good news down to her friends
from the highest car on the Ferris wheel.
                                    I wish amusement parks
didn't have such high admission prices. And, of course, I still like to eat.
Why just this morning I had a big bowl of cereal. The box says
you can get sixteen servings, but my husband and I never get more than ten,
        which makes each
serving about forty cents, not including the milk
or the banana or the glass of juice. But without that fuel,
who says I could have written this same poem? It may have been shorter
and even sadder, because I would have had a hunger headache
and not given it my best.
                        Then there's rent. I can't write this poem outside
as there are no plugs for my computer, and certainly no
surge protectors. I need to be comfortable—a sweatshirt and sweatpants,
which used to be cheaper before everyone started getting into fitness.
I need my glasses more than ever as I get older.
Without insurance, I don't have to tell you how expensive they are.
I need a pair of warm socks and a place to sleep.
Dreams are very important to poets. I need recreation, escape, Hollywood movies.
You may remember I made reference to one earlier called *Grease*,
lines 32–38 of this very poem.
                        It's not easy,
now that movies in New York are eight seventy-five.
You get in the theater and smell the buttered popcorn,
though everyone knows it's not really butter they use.
It's more like yellow-colored lard. Any poet with heart trouble
best skip it. But my husband and I smell it
and out come our wallets. The concession stand uses so much salt
every moviegoer also needs a drink, and everyone knows
what those prices are like. We say good-bye to another thirty bucks,
but that's just the beginning—
there are envelopes, bottles of Wite-Out, stamps, and disks.

Sex with a Famous Poet

I had sex with a famous poet last night
and when I rolled over and found myself beside him I shuddered
because I was married to someone else,
because I wasn't supposed to have been drinking,
because I was in a fancy hotel room
I didn't recognize. I would have told you
right off this was a dream, but recently
a friend told me, *write about a dream,*
lose a reader and I didn't want to lose you
right away. I wanted you to hear
that I didn't even like the poet in the dream, that he has
four kids, the youngest one my age, and I find him
rather unattractive, that I only met him once,
that is, in real life, and that was in a large group
in which I barely spoke up. He disgusted me
with his disparaging remarks about women.
He even used the word "Jap,"
which I took as a direct insult to my husband, who's Asian.
When we were first dating, I told him,
"You were talking in your sleep last night
and I listened, just to make sure you didn't
call out anyone else's name." My future husband said
that he couldn't be held responsible for his subconscious,
which worried me, which made me think his dreams
were full of blonde vixens in rabbit-fur bikinis,
but he said no, he dreamt mostly about boulders
and the ocean and volcanoes, dangerous weather
he witnessed but could do nothing to stop.
And I said, "I dream only of you,"
which was romantic and silly and untrue.
But I never thought I'd dream of another man—
my husband and I hadn't even had a fight,
my head tucked sweetly in his armpit, my arm
around his belly, which lifted up and down
all night, gently like water in a lake.
If I passed that famous poet on the street,
he would walk by, famous in his sunglasses
and blazer with the suede patches at the elbows,

without so much as a glance in my direction.
I know you're probably curious about who the poet is,
so I should tell you the clues I've left aren't
accurate, that I've disguised his identity,
that you shouldn't guess *I bet it's him* . . .
because you'll never guess correctly
and even if you do, I won't tell you that you have.
I wouldn't want to embarrass a stranger
who is, after all, probably a nice person,
who was probably just having a bad day when I met him,
who is probably growing a little tired of his fame—
which my husband and I perceive as enormous,
but how much fame can an American poet
really have, let's say, compared to a rock star
or film director of equal talent? Not that much,
and the famous poet knows it, knows that he's not
truly given his due. Knows that many
of these young poets tugging on his sleeve
are only pretending to have read all his books.
But he smiles anyway, tries to be helpful.
I mean, this poet has to have some redeeming qualities, right?
For instance, he writes a mean iambic.
Otherwise, what was I doing in his arms?

The Difference between Pepsi and Pope

I have this blind spot, a dark line, thin as a hair, that obliterates
a stroke of scenery on the right side of my field of vision
so that often I get whole words at the end of sentences wrong
like when I first saw the title of David Lehman's poem
"The Difference Between Pepsi and Coke" and I misread
"Coke" for "Pope." This blind spot makes me a terrible driver,
a bad judge of distances, a ping-pong player that inspires giggles
from the opposite team.
                              I knew a poet who dressed up as a cookie
and passed out a new brand in a crowded supermarket.
The next day he gave the Pepsi Challenge to passersby
in a mall.
                    I felt old-fashioned admitting to this poet that I prefer Coke,
that wavy hyphen that separates its full name Coca~Cola.
Like the bar let down in the limbo dance, the Spanish tilde comes down until
not even a lowercase letter can squeeze under it.
I searched for that character recently, writing to David Lehman,
telling him about an electronic magazine, the address of which
had this ~ in it. I couldn't find it, although I stared
at my computer keyboard for more than a few minutes.
I only noticed it today in the upper left hand corner, above the tab,
the alternate of ', if you hit the shift key. I wonder if I also have a blind spot
in my left eye. I wonder if the poet who dressed as a cookie
is happy in his new marriage. I wonder if you can still get a bottle of Tab
anywhere, that awful soda my forever-dieting aunt used to drink,
with its pink logo, its "a" all swirls, looking like @.
                                                          Yesterday,
when my husband was waiting at an intersection, he said, *Is anyone coming?* I
        looked from
the passenger seat and said confidently, *We can make it.*
Then we were almost run off the road. I said
I'm sorry I'm sorry through the exchange of honks and fists
and couldn't believe when my husband forgave me so quickly.
                                                          Not only that,
but I'm a bad proofreader, I thought to myself as I made a mental list
of ways that I felt inadequate. One friend also recently noted that maybe I
talk too much about myself, so I told her the Bette Midler joke,

Enough about me, what do you think of me? which doesn't *really*
bring me back to David Lehman and his poem, but does make me realize
how far away I strayed from my original point,
which was that I thought his poem would be funny because of the title,
not the real title, but my mistaken one. I started to guess his poem
in my head: Pepsi is bubbly and brown while the Pope
is flat and white. Pepsi doesn't have a big white hat. The Pope
can't get rid of fender rust. Pepsi is all for premarital sex.
The Pope won't stain your teeth.
                                But "The Difference
Between Pepsi and Coke" is a tender poem about a father
whom the speaker reveres and I wonder if David Lehman's own father
is alive or dead, which is something I often do—wonder
how much is true—when I read a poem by someone I like,
which I know is not the right way to read a poem even though
Molly Peacock said at her reading that she is the "I"
in all of hers and doesn't use the word "speaker" anymore.
                                                        Still,
I feel like a Peeping Tom, although this is really about what I can't see,
my blind spots, and how easy it is for me to doubt my decisions,
how I relate to the father in Lehman's poem who "won't admit his dread
of boredom" and panics and forgives. How easy it is to live for stretches at a time
in that skinny dark line, how easy it is to get so many things all wrong.

Yes

According to *Culture Shock:*
A Guide to Customs and Etiquette
of Filipinos, when my husband says yes,
he could also mean one of the following:
a.) *I don't know.*
b.) *If you say so.*
c.) *If it will please you.*
d.) *I hope I have said yes unenthusiastically enough*
for you to realize I mean no.
You can imagine the confusion
surrounding our movie dates, the laundry,
who will take out the garbage
and when. I remind him
I'm an American, that all his yeses sound alike to me.
I tell him here in America we have shrinks
who can help him to be less of a people-pleaser.
We have two-year-olds who love to scream "No!"
when they don't get their way. I tell him,
in America we have a popular book,
When I Say No I Feel Guilty.
"Should I get you a copy?" I ask.
He says yes, but I think he means
"If it will please you," i.e., "I won't read it."
"I'm trying," I tell him, "but you have to try too."
"Yes," he says, then makes *tampo*,
a sulking that the book *Culture Shock* describes as
"subliminal hostility . . . withdrawal of customary cheerfulness
in the presence of the one who has displeased" him.
The book says it's up to me to make things all right,
"to restore goodwill, not by talking the problem out,
but by showing concern about the wounded person's
well-being." Forget it, I think, even though I know
if I'm not nice, *tampo* can quickly escalate into *nagdadabog*—
foot stomping, grumbling, the slamming
of doors. Instead of talking to my husband, I storm off
to talk to my porcelain Kwan Yin,
the Chinese goddess of mercy
that I bought on Canal Street years before

my husband and I started dating.
"The real Kwan Yin is in Manila,"
he tells me. "She's called Nuestra Señora de Guia.
Her Asian features prove Christianity
was in the Philippines before the Spanish arrived."
My husband's telling me this
tells me he's sorry. Kwan Yin seems to wink,
congratulating me—my short prayer worked.
"Will you love me forever?" I ask,
then study his lips, wondering if I'll be able to decipher
what he means by his yes.

Bangungot

Ever since my husband told me about *bangungot*
and taught me how to say it—
three short nasally syllables, a cross between
banana and coconut—I've been worried
he's going to get it, that he'll die in his sleep.
Some Filipinos believe a demon who sits on a man's chest
or violent nightmares are the real killers.
My husband thinks it's too much
fish sauce or shrimp paste late at night,
that third helping of rice. *Bangungot*
strikes men 25–40, men who like to eat,
then snooze. I try not to let my husband do this
and suggest, instead of television, a walk after dinner,
a game of cards. But sometimes I have places to go.
Sometimes I fall asleep before he does.
It's then I dream of my husband's stomach—
a pot of rice boiling over, a banana so ripe
its own skin cracks. Or I fly, just from the waist up,
a *manananggal,* a vampire that can only be killed
with salt, a vampire who kills men in their sleep.
The top of my body leans into my husband's chest
and I demand he teach me to pronounce the word
that doesn't look like it's spelled. He is confused,
asks me *Where are your legs?*
By the time I get them back,
I'm a widow in black ballerina flats.

Nick at Nite

When growing up, Nick never saw *The Brady Bunch*.
He watched *Eat Bulaga* with Tito, Vic, and Joey,
which he likens to a Filipino version of *The Three Stooges*.
He ate Sky Flakes crackers instead of Ritz
and drank Royal True Orange with pulp bits instead of Sunkist.
He remembers the bells signaling the after-dinner arrival
of Magnolia ice cream–vendors pushing silver coolers,
not driving trucks. I tell him about Apple Jacks,
the cereal that turned a kid's milk pink
and the phenomenon of Banana Quik.
I try to explain Madge, the brassy beautician who dipped
her clients' hands in Palmolive Dishwashing Liquid
between manicures. My husband endures
the moving scrapbook of my childhood
as we watch another round of Nick at Nite.
I teach him all the words to the *Patty Duke Show* theme song
during a break from their sponsors Head & Shoulders.
In the Philippines, dandruff was also an embarrassment.
Nick tells me of a shampoo commercial in English and Tagalog:
A girl loses interest in her dancing partner
when she notices the white patches on his collar
and huffs away as only the truly insulted can.
The famous slogan: "Charlie Balakubak, excuse me!"
My husband and I laugh. We are "East Meets West"
like LaChoy, makers of "Oriental recipes to serve at home."
I sing him *"Ay yay ay yay* . . . I am the Frito Bandito."
Nick, who only started speaking English at six,
translates the original Spanish lyrics. The song, he says,
is really about singing without tears, not the virtues of corn chips.

Playa Naturista

We're brave, but we're not *that* brave
so we go in the morning, arrive by 8:30,
when any self-respecting vacationing Spaniard
would still be in bed sleeping. I take off
my bathing-suit top first and my breasts
are surprised by the sun, which they haven't seen
since they were seven or eight
when they were just nipples and seeds.
They blush pink on the empty beach
and I quickly turn over onto my stomach,
planning to stay there forever,
or at least until sundown. My husband
is in his swimming trunks, contemplating
how to get out of them—while standing up
or lying down. I look around,
suspiciously, wondering if all the other tourists
will have had implants, but it's still no one but us
and the occasional Mediterranean gull.

I close my eyes and listen to the ocean sounds—
sloshing, blood and heart, pulses,
stomach rumbles, whispering of lungs,
muscle flex, cold beer gulp, pumping,
pumping—the inside noises any body makes.

My husband nudges me and points.
The sun on the waves is a million
diamond rings. "Look," he says
as the grandma jogs by, in white sneakers
and a white visor, and nothing else.
Her breasts flop happily, her buttocks
jiggle like cove ripples. "*Hola!*"
she hollers, out of breath, all wrinkles
and sweat. She is the goddess
of nude bathing we've prayed to.
She says all bodies are beautiful
and made of water and love the sea.

My husband and I slip out of our bottoms
and run like Adam and Eve, if
Adam smoked Dunhills and Eve
wore Ray-Bans. Suddenly we're in the water
like brother and sister, like Adam and Eve
technically were. My breasts bob
like white apples, like I'm wearing a push-up bra
made of salt water. My husband
is swimming out further, at peace
with his shrinking penis that he forgets
all about because now we are dolphins
and the pleasure of water is everywhere,
swirling around each toe and pubic hair
with the same cool-womb delight.
We swim through each other's legs,
watch for fish that flash like silver
bracelets you can buy in the market.
Our fingernails are as white
as bleached bone or the stone buildings
of Mojácar. Our lips are salty and soft
and prickly as anchovies.

Our skin tightens around our bodies
as the sun moves higher in the sky.
We're having too much fun to notice.
Our watches are with our beach mats
and towels and umbrella.

When we finally look back
to the shore, we see families,
nude ones, with curly hair
and plastic pails and shovels
and Fanta Limón coolers.
We think we see a naked Jesus walk by,
the tanned hippy version
we grew up with. We see pot bellies
and stretch marks and scars.

We only hesitate a moment
before we rise out of the water, holding
each other's arms, tiptoeing on rough pebbles,
trying to keep our footing.
And we face them, all of them,
our bodies and theirs now
perfect and elegant. We are dripping
wet and full of wet tendrils,
my husband wearing only
his seaweed tie and I, a boa of kelp.

New Poems

Mia and Darger, Ashbery and Gina

When Mia saw my Darger poster, she said, "Oh wow! Look Patrick, Darger,"
and I couldn't believe she knew who he was. I thought I had discovered
him in La Collection de L'Art Brut in Switzerland.
But, of course, I couldn't have really discovered him
since there was already a poster and an expensive French coffee-table book
that I also bought at the Swiss museum and lugged home in my carry-on.
"Ashbery's next book is all about Darger," Mia quipped.
Mia worked at Farrar Straus & Giroux. I had known her for about one minute.
She was visiting because she'd come along with Patrick,
a friend of my husband's. I wished I hadn't cooked Mia pumpkin soup.
For a minute I hated her—I'd wanted *my* next book to be about Darger.
Then Patrick said, "Did you see the Darger show
here in New York last year?" And my dream of discovering Darger—
bringing him back to America like some strange spice—was over.
My husband was getting everyone drinks. I was frozen, processing,
that I didn't hate Mia or Patrick, mere messengers.

Who I hated was Ashbery
for having my idea first—for having the art world connections
to know about Darger, apparently years before I did. I wanted to be the one
to save the Chicago hospital janitor who wrote a 15,145 page novel
discovered only after his death, along with these amazing illustrations
(some of which are shown on my Darger poster) and, according to Mia and
     Patrick,
hung in museums around the world. Mia told me Darger *wasn't* retarded—
I'd mistranslated the French from my coffee-table book. She explained
he was mentally ill. I felt queasy in that schoolgirl way—*what was I thinking?*
Surely he couldn't have been retarded

and written 15,145 cohesive pages.
A few days later Mia sent me a Darger article written in English
and John Ashbery's new book, not the one about Darger
(it wasn't published yet) but the one called *Wakefulness.*
I wrote a poem called "Sleepyhead," which was probably some weird aggressive,
anti-Ashbery statement though I didn't know it at the time.
Ashbery was born in the same year as my dad. Ashbery looks
pretty much like my dad. My dad doesn't know who Ashbery is,
or, for that matter, Darger. My father never writes anything down—

he's only ever sent me one letter in my whole life, a thank you note
after he recovered from his surgery a few years ago.
I was suddenly angry at my dad for not being Ashbery
because then I would have had access to Darger earlier.
Or, if Ashbery were my father, I would have known more clearly,
earlier on, that I would never be crowned King
of the New York School.

My friend Tom said, "It's really a blessing
Ashbery got your, well, actually *his*, idea. It doesn't really sound like this Darger
guy is your thing." But Darger was exactly my thing—he drew little girls
with penises, he was obsessed with good and evil, he traced the Coppertone girl
for one of his drawings. I pierced a shrimp onto my fork
and noticed how much it looked like me when I go into the fetal position
after some disappointment (like this Darger/Ashbery thing).
I had to admit Ashbery got there first. I had to accept it,
just like I had to accept that my friend Nancy was the first
to get a pair of denim clogs with strawberry appliqués in eighth grade.
Sure, I could have also bought a pair of the same blue clogs, but everyone knew
Nancy was the cool one, the fashion genius, the one with the true what's-in flair.
It's not like I hadn't tried to gather more Darger information, to stay current.
Since I'd come back from Switzerland, I'd searched Netscape in vain,
tried to call the Darger Foundation in Chicago, which wasn't listed.
The article Mia sent explained the Foundation was called something else.
Anyway, here are some of the highlights from my Darger file:

HENRY DARGER (1892–1973)

Mother died when he was young and then, after his father
        fell ill, he was put in an orphanage and separated from his
        sister who was put in another orphanage . . .
violent storms in his work—maybe witnesses tornadoes as a kid?
gave his girl children penises (in illustrations only)

His novel is one of a struggle between nations on an
enormous planet of which earth is but a moon

Glandelians—practice child slavery (evil)

Abbiennia—good Christian nation

Blengins—colorful winged monsters that help sisters in their fight

Seven Vivian sisters fight Glandelians to free child slaves

Henry Darger appears as several characters, evil and good, and as
a war correspondent (In real life, H.D. had never been in a war. . . .)

In one story, sisters escape by rolling themselves into carpets
(see plate 1)

the closest thing he comes to sexual in his writing is "the
most delicate part of her legs" describing Little Jennie Anges
(child Martyr) tortured by G's and killed at age six holding
on so tightly to the Eucharist that they can't pry her hands
apart even when they hack away at the rest of her . . .

Well, you get the picture. I'll probably go back and delete that file,
drag the whole thing to the trash can icon and watch it bloat.
I wonder if I'm up to a Darger biography, if the Darger Foundation
would let me do it. I wonder if TNT would be interested in a mini-series
starring Nicholas Cage as Darger. But if Ashbery's already written the poems,
I'm sure someone else has already thought of these projects.
And then there's that whole thing about appropriation,
which I've gotten into trouble with before.

                                    Did you hear about that guy
Tony Kaye who directed (but now hates) *American History X*
because he says it was all chopped up in the editing room?
Well, before he directed this film, he exhibited a homeless man
in London's Tate Gallery. The man wore a sign around his neck
that read "BY TONY KAYE." I mean, believe me, I know it's grotesque
on a human level—I'm not disputing that. But I thought it was
kind of an interesting idea—how artists take the suffering of others

(Darger, our friends, people we pass on the street)
and try to make it art.

                I always wondered which part
of the body decomposed fastest until Gina told me last week, "The tongue
is the first thing to go." I had been explaining to her about teeth
and how they last even longer than bones. Gina's telling me
about the tongue made me really sad, though this sadness
seemed to have nothing to do with Gina's dead husband
or her little girl who looked like one of the Vivian sisters
in Darger's illustrations. She kept stooping to write her name Natasia
with a stick in the sand on the horse path in Central Park
as Nick walked ahead with our other friends Lara and Eric.
The rollerbladers zoomed in circles to disco music.
The actor Kevin Bacon held his child up on his shoulder
and his wife Kyra Sedgewick seemed to smile at us, especially at Natasia.
All I could think about was Darger—
not about his compulsive tracing of little girls,
not about Kevin Bacon playing him in a full-length movie,
not about how, if I was bold enough, I could walk up to him right then
and pitch my idea.

                All I could think about was Darger's by-now
decomposed tongue. I was afraid my father would die soon,
because now he needed more surgery. I was afraid he would die,
what with his lack of interest in writing, something I always imagined
could help people live longer. I wished that my father would leave
a 15,145 page novel behind in the garage so that I could discover something
about his life that I hadn't noticed when he was busy working
and being my dad. Gina was in the process of editing
her dead husband's novel. No one knew how to talk to her about it.
She hated when people asked things like, "So how are you doing?"
How did they think she was doing, having just buried such a young husband?
Gina herself looked like a teenager, her daughter's big sister.
My father looked like Ashbery, but maybe a little younger,
maybe like Ashbery's little brother.

I showed a picture of my dad
to Mia. "He looks like Ashbery, doesn't he?" I asked.
Mia bit into a sweet wiry piece of baklava and nodded.
Later she said she was thinking about doing an anthology all about science.
I didn't want to tell her, but I had to mention *Verse & Universe,*
edited by Kurt Brown, just out with Milkweed.
Her face fell just like mine did when she told me
about Ashbery and Darger.

"Maybe you can still do a book, I mean,
Ashbery's not *directly* writing about Darger. . . ." Mia had said,
trying to cheer me up.

"Maybe you can still do an anthology, Mia. . . ."
I was saying now. "Maybe you could just focus on technology
or math or physics."

And I really felt bad for Mia, for not getting her idea
in time. I really felt bad for Darger, for Natasia, and especially for Gina,
who I hope doesn't accuse me of being a Tony Kaye for putting her
and her daughter in this poem. I said something not very articulate to Mia
about the effects of suffering being pointless without religion or art.
Patrick and my husband looked up from their coffee cups,
and at the same time both said, "What are you two talking about?"

Ego

I just didn't get it—
even with the teacher holding an orange (the earth) in one hand
and a lemon (the moon) in the other,
her favorite student (the sun) standing behind her with a flashlight.
I just couldn't grasp it—
this whole citrus universe, these bumpy planets revolving so slowly
no one could even see themselves moving.
I used to think if I could only concentrate hard enough
I could be the one person to feel what no one else could,
sense a small tug from the ground, a sky shift, the earth changing gears.
Even though I was only one minispeck on a speck,
even though I was merely a pinprick in one goosebump on the orange,
I was sure then I was the most specially perceptive, perceptively sensitive.
I was sure then my mother was the only mother to snap—
"The world doesn't revolve around you!"
The earth was fragile and mostly water
just the way the orange was mostly water if you peeled it
just the way I was mostly water if you peeled me.
Looking back on that third-grade science demonstration,
I can understand why some people gave up on fame or religion or cures—
especially people who have an understanding
of the excruciating crawl of the world,
who have a well-developed sense of spatial reasoning
and the tininess that it is to be one of us.
But not me—even now I wouldn't mind being god, the force
who spins the planets the way I spin a globe, a basketball, a yo-yo.
I wouldn't mind being that teacher who chooses the fruit,
or that favorite kid who gives the moon its glow.

Superego

A few days ago I wrote this poem "Ego,"
and when I showed it to my husband, he said,
"Satan went to hell for wanting to be God, you know. . . .
Remember Lucifer?" He laughed, half
sort of believing in hell and half not.
I tried to look smart, paraphrasing John Gardner,
who wrote about how for a while the third person omniscient
went out of fashion because no writers wanted to be God
and/or no one believed in Him anymore anyway.
By Him with a capital "H," I mean God.
Not many writers believe in God,
but they still believe in Gardner.

A while ago my friend Maureen Seaton and I
made this prosepoem "Hemisphere" in which I wrote:

> *I am trying to be an omniscient narrator like God, who supposedly can be*
> *inside your mind and outside at the same time. That's why most humans*
> *write in the first person—because they are not God although most humans*
> *don't write at all except for grocery lists and postcards.*

Then Maureen wrote:

> *Since I read what I wrote about God, I have experienced a tinker of my*
> *brain or a tinker in my brain—and that tinker, the noun, is you, the*
> *omniscient narrator in the second person.*

I was the one to bring up God in the poem, but Maureen and I try to find
this third voice when we collaborate so we're sort of mushed into one,
sort of, I suppose, a chorus. Sort of the opposite of God.

We wrote the poem "Hemisphere" before I read John Gardner's book,
before I read what John Gardner said about how imperative
it is for writers to read everything so that we don't repeat great ideas
in a lesser way. I suppose that's what happened with "Hemisphere."
John Gardner already had the idea about the writer being god
at least two decades earlier. But I'm glad at least Maureen
took the idea further. She's probably never read Gardner,
because she's not interested in writing prose. I'm still thinking about "Ego,"

that whole thing about the moon being a lemon—does it even work?
It's really sort of hard to write about the moon
unless you're Michael Burkard. He has this great line—
one gets more used to the moon when one knows one is a piece of it.
Or what about Lorca—
. . . an incomprehensible moon illuminating dried lemon rinds . . .
My husband Nick says Lorca's moon is even better in Spanish.
In one of his own poems, Nick tries
to figure out which language does the moon the most justice—
. . . la luna, la lua, la lune, ang buwan . . .

Now I'm embarrassed that three of my favorite moon references
are by male poets. Part of me wants to hop up
and scour my books to find three female poets
with something equally enchanting to say about the moon.
But another part of me thinks that's cheating,
like when people add epigraphs *after* they've finished a poem.
I'd be too scared to do it, embarrassed that someone
would find out. I get embarrassed a lot lately. I blushed
all through Ellen Hinsey's essay, "The Rise of Modern Doggerel,"
in which she claims, more or less,
that most contemporary personal poems,
the ones with the "therapeutic I," are pathetic.
I felt sick when I read that essay, sure she was talking about me
and all my therapeutic poems.
(See poem written a few days ago, "Ego.")

Later I was embarrassed when I saw the woman
who suggested I read the essay in the first place.
I mean, I felt that same sort of shame that I had
reading Gardner's *The Art of Fiction* on the subway.
A student/writer–type sitting on the orange seat next to me
asked me if I was reading Gardner because I was trying to write a novel.
The truth was I'd already finished the novel
and was reading the book to see where I'd gone wrong.
I felt like everything was going backwards, like the subway itself
was backing up and I was getting younger instead of older,
like every poem I'd ever written was unraveling into meaningless syllables.

I started taking advice from this undergraduate from NYU
who was sure he was sitting on a best-seller.

I started telling him about the moon, how I have about twenty-five drafts
of the same poem, trying to write about the time
when my sister and her husband were out of town
and my niece and I slept in the same bed,
her breathing a small wind-up toy,
her curls crunched between her face and pillow
carving curlicue sleep lines on her cheek.
The poem was like "The Rise of Modern Doggerel" itself
when she woke me up at three in the morning
because she couldn't see the moon through the window.
"It's out there," I promised, but my niece explained
she really *needed* to see it. More than anything in the world,
she needed something to drink and needed
the moon. She drank tap water from her favorite cup,
then I lifted her onto my hip so her feet wouldn't be cold.
I stood in the driveway in a small town in Rhode Island
where the moon was a communion wafer poker chip
and as white as my niece's milk teeth,
as white as the whites of her eyes.

I wasn't afraid then of hell or god. My niece was sure
Jesus was a girl because His pajamas looked like girl pajamas.
Whenever I held her, I didn't even care about poems.
I wanted her to believe that Jesus was a girl.
I hadn't yet met that NYU student who I let intimidate me.
I hadn't even heard of John Gardner.
The driveway, the moon, my niece's Care Bear pajamas.
I didn't know then Care Bear cartoons came *after* the Care Bears,
that Care Bear cartoons were really sinister
commercials to sell the pajamas et al.
It was just the alabaster moon, a little girl, and a young woman.
It was definitely one of those "therapeutic I" moments.
A moment that would have reminded Gardner
of a much better literary moment, maybe something
that Shakespeare wrote about with more flair.

A moment that would have made Ellen Hinsey shudder.
A moment the NYU student would have been too busy to notice,
what with his big novel to revise.
My niece was so little then, with a little ego.
She said, "I love you, moon!"
then the moon said, "I love you, too."

Id

(for Lexia)

I'm having coffee at the Last Stop with Amy
who tells me about her teaching—
she teaches adjunct composition even though she has a PhD
just like my friend Page. Amy says her students at FIT
really love Sylvia Plath—
The moon sees nothing of this. She is bald and wild.
The line falls off her tongue like rain or salt,
something easy and helpful.
It's the day after *Prairie Schooner* has accepted "Superego"
(even though when I originally wrote it, it had the title
"The Other Day I Wrote This Poem Ego"). It was Amy's idea
to change the title—and I think she was right,
especially because it is a companion poem
to this other poem "Ego" and now to this poem "Id."

In the poem "Superego," I presented this moral,
or rather, this to-revise-or-not-to-revise dilemma:
should I go back to change the lines in which I can
only think of men who write about the moon?
Should I plug in Sylvia Plath's lines as if I knew them
without looking them up? As a poet, I just want my reader
to trust me. Would they believe I actually knew all those lines by heart?
I'd just been reading an article about memoir writing
that cautioned memoirists against using dialogue—
if you really want your reader to believe you,
you shouldn't use artifice, you shouldn't write,
Then Mommy said and launch into a paragraph of her exact words
since no one has a memory like that. Rather, the author
of the article advised, you should paraphrase.

I used to try to teach my composition students to paraphrase
when I taught at Baruch College, the same place where Page teaches now—
I'd give them a paragraph, but they'd just basically copy the whole thing
changing one or two words like "carry" to "lift up." Anyway, the truth is
I should have known those Plath lines, and as soon as Amy said them,
I did. I even remembered some other lines—

The moon is no door. It is a face in its own right,
White as a knuckle and terribly upset.
There was a time when I was obsessed by Plath, so when Amy tells me
Meg Ryan has just bought the movie rights to tell Plath's story,
we both agree—"Bleck! What next? Ted Hughes played by Tom Hanks?"
But who knows, maybe Meg is obsessed with Plath like I was
when I visited Smith College and looked through Sylvia's papers
and the little hairs on my arms bristled with electricity
the same way they did when I saw my first dead body.
My eyes grew all moist and blurry when I saw her juvenilia,
her "Angel with Guitar" drawn in colored pencil, so sappy
a picture I knew she must have been happy when she drew it.
Maybe Meg Ryan will do a good job.

The picture was before any of Sylvia's poems.
My trip to Smith was before Sylvia's lines settled like dust bunnies
under the couch in my brain, before I'd lost Plath's moon that
drags the sea after it like a dark crime. I'm always forgetting
not only lines of poems, but names and phone numbers
and where I put my keys. I forget the facts of stories
I thought I knew. For example, the other night,
after I read another one of my poems
"The Difference between Pepsi and Pope" at a reading,
my friend Page came up to me and said,
"Hey, don't you remember? I was that cookie!"
(I'd referred to a poet whose job it was to dress up like a cookie in a mall.)
"Why did you turn me into a man?" she asked. The thing was
I was sure the person in the cookie costume was Michael Burkard
when I wrote the poem, so I made the cookie a he.
I didn't want to use Michael's real name
because I hadn't been in touch with him
in a long time and I thought maybe he wouldn't want
anyone to know about his cookie-dressing days.
Besides, it was such good material I thought
he might want to use it for a poem of his own.

But the real story, Page reminded me,
is that while she dressed up as a cookie in a mall in Maryland

to pass out free samples to shopping customers,
Michael would come by to visit her since he lived in the neighborhood.
All those years I had Michael's head on top
of a chocolate chip–speckled body, but now I've corrected it
in my mind, now Page's head is there instead.
More than ever, I think it's about time Page got a really good job,
one with tenure and sabbaticals and even an expense account.
Maybe Amy could teach in the sister school and only have to go in
twice a week. I wish this poem could serve as a recommendation letter
for Page and Amy, or introductory letter for myself
since I adjunct as well. I wish the three of us had big jobs
with pension and dental plans. I first became aware
of Page when I read one of her poems
in *Prairie Schooner* in the mid-eighties. It was a great poem,
I read it over and over again, and it finally dawned on me
that she was the same Page whose mailbox "Delano" at Baruch
was right above mine. I wrote her a fan letter and we became friends.

At the reception for the reading,
Stephanie and Kathy (or Stephanie or Kathy) said Page
should change her name to Lexia, the name for a page in hypertext.
My friend Amy (with whom I'm sipping coffee
at the Last Stop, remember?) is explaining why she didn't make the reading.
I tell her her friend Shira was there. Shira's blonde hair
hung like a shiny shawl over her arm as she looked at the cookies
and wondered if she should have one. I opted for Chex mix
and apple juice because I knew if I had sugar
my head would start racing even faster than it already was,
talking to my friends whom I hadn't seen since before Christmas.
Marcia's mother had Alzheimer's, just like Nick's.
I was trying to set up Scott to run this reading series.
I'd just missed Mark's reading, which made me feel bad.
I'd just met Kate Light and Johanna Keller. I'd just heard Pat Mangan
read for the first time. Stephanie asked him if he was related
to a famous Mangan and he was. I looked again at Shira's long hair
since I was getting my hair cut short the next week
and was starting to have serious doubts.

Someone turned the lights on and off, meaning the reception was over.
Someone came and took away the Chex Mix and picked up
the empty paper cups. Stephanie and I got our coats.
Since we were both reading with Pat,
we were supposed to have traveled together to the West Village
but we had missed each other
at the Lexington station where the N (my line) meets the 6
(the train Stephanie takes). We were supposed to meet at the escalator,
but there are at least three escalators at that stop so I ran back and forth
between the ones I saw while Stephanie waited
at the only one she knew of (which was the one I couldn't find).
Anyway, we both gave up after half an hour
and took the N then the 1 and met instead on Christopher Street.
We'd given up exactly at the same time, we'd talked to the same set
of policemen at Lexington Station. We just began walking
toward Barrow Street as though it were unremarkable.
But it was pretty remarkable, the way the timing went,
the way we were probably on the same trains.

On the way home, we got off at Lexington again and found the escalator
where Stephanie had waited—there was actually a set,
one going up and one going down with a flight of stairs
in the middle. It was on the opposite side of one of the platforms
where I'd waited. I realize now, as this poem comes to a close,
that it's sort of New York School
the way I put in the names of my friends. When I told David
I was working on a poem called "Id," he said that I should
only use words that contain the letters "id," maybe even
put his name in the title, "(Dav)ID." Even though
he was only kidding, I considered
his idea for a minute—then this sentence
would have instead read "Kidding considered idea."
I like language techniques and surrealist games, but the truth is
I'm always trying to say something, I'm always that earnest kid
with her hand up, with an idea the teacher
has to help her sputter out. I'm really sorry
I mixed Page up with Michael, even though Page
says she doesn't care. Amy's really sorry

she didn't make the reading because she's never heard Stephanie before.
Did I mention Stephanie is a wiz at hypertext?
If I were one, too, there'd be these links to help you
get through "Id." For example, you'd click on the word Page
and it would take you back to the dedication.

Acknowledgments

Poems in *Queen for a Day* were originally published in: *Smile!* (Warm Spring Press, 1993—out of print now but available online at the Contemporary American Poetry Archive at http://capa.conncoll.edu/index.html); *The Woman with Two Vaginas*, winner of the Salmon Run Poetry Prize, (Salmon Run Press, 1995—out of print but also online at http://capa.conncoll.edu/index.html); *Girl Soldier* (Garden Street Press, 1996); *How the Sky Fell*, winner of Pearl Editions' chapbook contest, (Pearl Editions, 1996); *Kinky* (Orchises Press, 1997); and *The Star-Spangled Banner*, winner of the Crab Orchard Award in Poetry, (Southern Illinois University Press, 1999). Thanks to these presses.

Grateful acknowledgment is made to the editors of the following magazines in which these poems first appeared: *Asian Pacific American Journal* ("Bangungot"); *Artful Dodge* ("How the Sky Fell"); *Brooklyn Review* ("Whole"); *Chicago Review* ("Bisexual Barbie"); *Confluence* ("The Hollow Men"); *Controlled Burn* ("Nick at Nite," under the title "Swing American"); *Crab Orchard Review* ("Yes"); *Folio* ("Barbie's GYN Appointment" and "Barbie Joins a Twelve Step Program"); *Footwork* ("Summer" and "Oriental Barbie"); *Free Lunch* ("The Woman with Two Vaginas"); *Hanging Loose* ("Feminism"); *Journal of Progressive Human Social Services* ("The Raping of the Sun"); *Long Shot* ("How to Help Children through Wartime"); *Mudfish* ("David Lemieux" and "When I Was a Lesbian"); *The National Poetry Magazine of the Lower East Side* ("Marriage"); *North Dakota Quarterly* ("Sometimes the First Boys Don't Count"); *One Mead Way* ("From the Shore"); *Ontario Review* ("Making Money," "The Ugly Stepsister," "June 13, 1995," and "Cockroaches"); *Poet Lore* ("Literary Barbie"); *Private* ("Barbie as Religious Fanatic"); *Poetry New York* ("Sex with a Famous Poet"); *Salt Hill Review* ("The Difference between Pepsi and Pope"); *Shattered Wig Review* ("Him-Whose-Penis-Never-Slept");

Sheila Na-Gig ("How Much Is This Poem Going to Cost Me?"); *Third Coast* (*"Playa Naturista"*); *West Coast Magazine* ("My Grandmother Is My Husband"); *West Branch* ("Four Hours"); and *Western Humanities Review* ("Blue Beard's One-Hundredth Wife").

Poems from the New Poems section first appeared in: *Indiana Review* ("Mia and Darger, Ashbery and Gina") and *Prairie Schooner* ("Ego," "Superego," and "Id," which were awarded the magazine's 1999 Strousse Award). With thanks to Brian Leung and Hilda Raz.

"Bulimia" was reprinted in *The Best American Poetry 1994* (Scribners) and *Literature around the Globe* (Kendall/Hunt, 1994). "Reminded of My Biological Clock—While Looking at Georgia O'Keeffe's *Pelvis One*" was reprinted in *Bearing Life: Women's Writings on Childlessness* (The Feminist Press, 2000). "Four Hours" was reprinted in *What's Become of Eden: Poems of Family at Century's End* (Slapering Hol Press, 1994). "Feminism" was reprinted in *The Best American Poetry 1993* (Scribners) and *Boomer Girls: American Women Poets Come of Age* (University of Iowa Press, 1999). "Fear on 11th Street and Avenue A, New York City" was reprinted in *Aloud: Voices from the Nuyorican Poets Café* (Henry Holt, 1994). "Kinky" first appeared in *Mondo Barbie* (St. Martin's Press, 1993) and was reprinted in *Between the Cracks—The Daedalus Anthology of Kinky Verse* (Daedalus Press, 1996) and *American Poetry: Next Generation* (Carnegie Mellon University Press, 2000) along with the poem "Yes." "Marriage" was reprinted in *The Year's Best Fantasy and Horror, Eleventh Annual Collection* (St. Martin's Press, 1998). "The Difference between Pepsi and Pope" was reprinted in *The Best American Poetry 1998* (Scribners) and *Jahrbuch der Lyrik 2001* (Verlag Beck, Munich, 2001). "Sex with a Famous Poet," "How Much Is This Poem Going to Cost Me?" and "Ego" were reprinted in *New Young American Poets* (Southern Illinois University Press, 2000). "Sex with a Famous Poet" is also reprinted in *The KGB Bar Book of Poems* (William Morrow & Co., 2000).

Much obliged to The MacDowell Colony, Yaddo, Villa Montalvo Center for the Arts, La Château de Lavigny (Lausanne, Switzerland), and Fundación Valparaíso (Almeria, Spain) for enchanting places to write; and to the Ludwig Vogelstein Foundation, the New York

Foundation for the Arts, and *Prairie Schooner*. A big thanks to Nick Carbó, Tom Fink, Rebecca McClanahan, Ed Ochester, Maureen Seaton, and especially Stephanie Strickland for all their help in suggesting poems to be included from earlier books.

Denise Duhamel's *Queen for a Day* includes poems from her five previous full-length books (*The Star-Spangled Banner, Kinky, Girl Soldier, The Woman with Two Vaginas,* and *Smile!*) as well as her chapbook *How the Sky Fell.*

Duhamel grew up in Woonsocket, Rhode Island, and was educated at Emerson College, where she received her B.F.A. degree, and Sarah Lawrence College, where she earned her M.F.A. degree. Her poems have been anthologized widely and have appeared in four editions of *The Best American Poetry* (2000, 1998, 1994, and 1993). Her work has been featured on NPR's "All Things Considered" and PBS's "Fooling with Words." She has collaborated with the poet Maureen Seaton on two volumes, *Oyl* and *Exquisite Politics.*

A recipient of a 2001 NEA fellowship, Denise Duhamel is an assistant professor at Florida International University in Miami. She is married to the poet Nick Carbó.

Photo by Nick Carbó